Life on the Golden Horn

The Turkish Empire, 1718

MARY WORTLEY MONTAGU

Life on the Golden Horn

GREAT
JOURNEYS

PENGUIN BOOKS

Published by the Penguin Group
Penguin Books Ltd, 80 Strand, London WC2R ORL, England
Penguin Group (USA) Inc., 375 Hudson Street, New York, New York 10014, USA
Penguin Group (Canada), 90 Eglinton Avenue East, Suite 700, Toronto, Ontario, Canada M4P 2Y3
(a division of Pearson Penguin Canada Inc.)
Penguin Ireland, 25 St Stephen's Green, Dublin 2, Ireland (a division of Penguin Books Ltd)
Penguin Group (Australia), 250 Camberwell Road, Camberwell, Victoria 3124, Australia
(a division of Pearson Australia Group Pty Ltd)
Penguin Books India Pvt Ltd, 11 Community Centre, Panchsheel Park, New Delhi – 110 017, India
Penguin Group (NZ), 67 Apollo Drive, Mairangi Bay, Auckland 1310, New Zealand
(a division of Pearson New Zealand Ltd)
Penguin Books (South Africa) (Pty) Ltd, 24 Sturdee Avenue, Rosebank, Johannesburg 2196, South Africa

Penguin Books Ltd, Registered Offices: 80 Strand, London WC2R ORL, England

www.penguin.com

Lady Mary Wortley Montagu's letters written 1716–1718
This extract published in Penguin Books 2007

1

All rights reserved

Inside-cover maps by Jeff Edwards

Typeset by Rowland Phototypesetting Ltd, Bury St Edmunds, Suffolk
Printed in England by Clays Ltd, St Ives plc

ISBN: 978-0-141-02542-1

Lady Mary Wortley Montagu (1689–1762) travelled to Constantinople in 1716 with her husband, who had been appointed ambassador there by the new Hanoverian king, George I. The embassy was a total failure and they were rapidly recalled. By contrast, Lady Mary's brilliant letters recounting her experience form one of the great travelogues of their period and are an overwhelmingly enjoyable record of a spectacular court and its customs.

This selection recounts her journey across Europe, her time in Vienna, the crossing of south-east Europe – utterly devastated by the long war between Austria and Turkey – and her arrival in first Adrianople (Edirne) and then Constantinople. The 'Rascians' mentioned in the text were mainly Croat and Serb troops settled on the military frontier to fight against the Turks. Her correspondents are mainly friends or influential acquaintances, including her sister Lady Mar and Alexander Pope.

Rotterdam, 3 August 1716

To Lady Mar,

I flatter myself, dear sister, that I shall give you some pleasure in letting you know that I am safely past the sea, though we had the ill fortune of a storm. We were persuaded by the captain of our yacht to set out in a calm, and he pretended that there was nothing so easy as to tide it over; but, after two days slowly moving, the wind blew so hard that none of the sailors could keep their feet and we were all Sunday night tossed very handsomely. I never saw a man more frighted than the captain. For my part I have been so lucky neither to suffer from fear or sea-sickness, though I confess I was so impatient to see myself once more upon dry land that I would not stay till the yacht could get to Rotterdam, but went in the long boat to Helvoetsluys, where we hired voitures to carry us to the Briel. I was charmed with the neatness of this little town, but my arrival in Rotterdam presented me a new scene of pleasure. All the streets are paved with broad stones, and before the meanest artificers' doors seats of various coloured marbles, and so neatly kept that, I'll assure you, I walked almost all over the town yesterday, in-cognito, in my slippers, without receiving one spot of dirt, and you may see the Dutch maids washing the pavement of the street with more application than ours do our bedchambers. The town seems so full of people, with such busy faces, all in motion, that I can hardly fancy that it is not some celebrated fair, but I see it is every day the same. 'Tis certain no town can be more advantageously situated for commerce. Here are seven large canals, on which the merchant ships come up to the very doors of their houses. The shops and warehouses are of a surprising neatness and magnificence, filled with an incredible quantity of fine merchandise, and so much cheaper than what we see in England I have much ado to persuade myself I am still so near it. Here is neither dirt nor beggary to be seen. One is not shocked with those loathsome cripples so common in London, nor teased with the importunities of idle fellows and wenches that choose to be nasty and lazy. The common servants and the little shop women here are more nicely clean than most of our ladies, and the great variety of neat dresses (every woman dressing her head after her own fashion) is an additional pleasure in seeing the town.

You see, hitherto, dear sister, I make no complaints, and if I continue to like travelling as well as I do at present, I shall not repent my project. It will go a great way in making me satisfied with it, if it affords me opportunities of entertaining you. But it is not from Holland that you must expect a disinterested offer. I can write enough in the style of Rotterdam to tell you plainly, in one word, that I expect returns of all the London news. You see I have already learnt to make a good bargain, and that it is not for nothing I will so much as tell you that I am your affectionate sister.

Vienna, 8 September 1716

To Lady Mar,

I am now, my dear sister, safely arrived at Vienna, and I thank God, have not at all suffered in my health, nor (what is dearer to me) in that of my child, by all our fatigues. We travelled by water from Ratisbon [Regensburg], a journey perfectly agreeable, down the Danube in one of those little vessels that they very properly call wooden houses, having in them all the conveniences of a palace, stoves in the chambers, kitchens etc. They are rowed by twelve men each and move with such incredible swiftness that in the same day you have the pleasure of a vast variety of prospects, and within a few hours space of time one has the pleasure of seeing a populous city adorned with magnificent palaces and the most romantic solitudes, which appear distant from the commerce of mankind, the banks of the Danube being charmingly diversified with woods, rocks, mountains covered with vines, fields of corn, large cities and ruins of ancient castles. I saw the great towns of Passau and Lintz, famous for the retreat of the imperial court when Vienna was besieged.

This town, which has the honour of being the Emperor's residence, did not at all answer my ideas of it, being much less than I expected to find it. The streets are very close, and so narrow one cannot observe the fine fronts of the palaces, though many of them very well deserve observation, being truly magnificent, all built of fine white stone and excessive high. The town being so much too little for the number of the people that desire to live in it, the builders seem to have projected to repair that misfortune by clapping one town on the top of another, most of the houses being of five and some of them six, storeys. You may easily imagine that the streets being so narrow, the upper rooms are extreme dark and, what is an inconvenience much more intolerable in my opinion, there is no house that has so few as five or six families in it. The apartments of the greatest ladies and even of the ministers of state, are divided but by a partition, from that of a tailor or shoemaker, and I know nobody that has above two floors in any house, one for their own use and one higher for their servants. Those that have houses of their own let out the rest of them to whoever will take them, thus the great stairs (which are all of stone) are as common and as dirty as the street. 'Tis true, when you have once travelled through them, nothing can be more surprisingly magnificent than the apartments. They are commonly a suite of eight or ten large rooms, all inlaid, the doors and windows richly carved and gilt and the furniture such as is seldom seen in the palaces of sovereign princes in other countries: the hangings of the finest tapestry of Brussels, prodigious large looking glasses in silver frames, fine Japan tables, beds, chairs, canopies and window curtains of the richest Genoa damask or velvet, almost covered with gold lace or embroidery, the whole made gay by pictures, and vast jars of japan china, and almost in every room large lustres of rock crystal.

I have already had the honour of being invited to

dinner by several of the first people of quality, and I must do them justice to say, the good taste and magnificence of their tables very well answers to that of their furniture. I have been more than once entertained with fifty dishes of meat, all served in silver, and well dressed; the dessert proportionable, served in the finest china. But the variety and richness of their wines is what appears the most surprising. The constant way is to lay a list of their names upon the plates of the guests along with the napkins, and I have counted several times to the number of eighteen different sorts, all exquisite in their kinds.

I was yesterday at Count Schönborn's, the vice-Chancellor's garden, where I was invited to dinner, and I must own that I never saw a place so perfectly delightful as the Fauxbourg of Vienna. It is very large, and almost wholly composed of delicious palaces, and if the emperor found it proper to permit the gates of the town to be laid open, that the Fauxbourg might be joined to it, he would have one of the largest and best built cities in Europe. Count Schönborn's villa is one of the most magnificent; the furniture all rich brocades, so well fancied and fitted up, nothing can look more gay and splendid, not to speak of a gallery full of rarities of coral, mother of pearl etc., and throughout the whole house a profusion of gilding, carving, fine paintings, the most beautiful porcelain statues of alabaster and ivory, and vast orange and lemon trees in gilt pots. The dinner was perfectly fine and well ordered, and made still more agreeable by the good humour of the count. I have not yet been at court, being forced to stay for my gown, without which there is no waiting on the Empress, though I am not without a great impatience to see a beauty that has been the admiration of so many different nations. When I have had that honour I will not fail to let you know my real thoughts, always taking a particular pleasure in communicating them to my dear sister.

Vienna, 14 September 1716

To Lady Mar,

Though I have so lately troubled you, dear sister, with a long letter, yet I will keep my promise in giving you an account of my first going to court. In order to that ceremony, I was squeezed up in a gown, and adorned with a gorget and the other implements thereunto belonging; a dress very inconvenient, but which certainly shows the neck and shape to great advantage. I cannot forbear in this place giving you some description of the fashions here, which are more monstrous and contrary to all common sense and reason than 'tis possible for you to imagine. They build certain fabrics of gauze on their heads, about a yard high, consisting of three or four storeys, fortified with numberless yards of heavy ribbon. The foundation of this structure is a thing they call a bourlé, which is exactly of the same shape and kind, but about four times as big as those rolls our prudent milk-maids make use of to fix their pails upon. This machine they cover with their own hair, which they mix with a great deal of false, it being a particular beauty to have their heads too large to go into a moderate tub. Their hair is prodigiously powdered to conceal the mixture and set out with three or four rows of bodkins (wonderfully large, that stick out two or three inches from their hair) made of diamonds, pearls, red, green and yellow stones, that it certainly requires as much art and experience to carry the load upright as to dance upon May day with the garland. Their whalebone petticoats out-do ours by several yards' circumference and cover some acres of ground. You may easily suppose how much this extraordinary dress sets off and improves the natural ugliness with which God Almighty has been pleased to endow them all generally. Even the lovely Empress herself is obliged to comply, in some degree, with these absurd fashions, which they would not quit for all the world.

I had a private audience, according to ceremony, of half an hour, and then all the other ladies were permitted to come make their court. I was perfectly charmed with the Empress; I cannot however tell you that her features are regular. Her eyes are not large, but have a lively look full of sweetness, her complexion the finest I ever saw, her nose and forehead well made but her mouth has ten thousand charms that touch the soul. When she smiles, 'tis with a beauty and sweetness that forces adoration. She has a vast quantity of fine fair hair; but then her person! One must speak of it poetically to do it rigid justice; all that the poets have said of the mien of Juno, the air of Venus, come not up to the truth. The Graces move with her; the famous statue of Medicis was not formed with more delicate proportions; nothing can be added to the beauty of her neck and hands. Till I saw them, I did not believe there were any in nature so perfect, and I was almost sorry that my rank here did not permit me to kiss them; but they are kissed sufficiently, for everybody that waits on her, pays that homage at their entrance and when they take leave. When the ladies were come in, she sat down to quinze. I could not play at a game I had never seen before, and she ordered me a seat at her right hand, and had the goodness to talk to me very much, with that grace so natural to her. I expected every moment when the men were to come in to pay their court, but this drawing room is very different from that of England. No man enters it but the old grand master, who comes in to advertise the Empress of the approach of the Emperor. His imperial majesty did me the honour of speaking to me in a very obliging manner, but he never speaks to any of the other ladies and the whole passes with a gravity and air of ceremony that has something very formal in it. The Empress Amelia, dowager of the late Emperor Joseph, came this evening to wait on the reigning Empress, followed by the two Archduchesses her daughters, who are very agreeable young princesses. Their imperial majesties rise and go to meet her at the door of the room, after which she is seated in an armed chair next the Empress, and in the same manner at supper, and there the men have the permission of paying their court. The Archduchesses sit on chairs with backs without arms. The table is entirely served, and all the dishes set on by the Empress' maids of honour, which are twelve young ladies of the first quality. They have no salary but their chambers at court, where they live in a sort of confinement, not being suffered to go to the assemblies or public places in town, except in complement to the wedding of a sister maid, whom the empress always presents with her picture set in diamonds. The three first of them are called ladies of the key, and wear gold keys by their sides; but what I find most pleasant is the custom which obliges them as long as they live after they have left the Empress' service, to make her some present every year on the day of her feast. Her majesty is served by no married woman but the *grande maitresse*, who is generally a widow of the first quality, always very old, and is at the same time groom of the stole, and mother of the maids. The dressers are not at all in the figure they pretend to in England, being looked upon no otherwise than as downright chambermaids.

I had an audience the next day of the Empress Mother, a princess of great virtue and goodness, but who piques herself so much on a violent devotion she is perpetually performing extraordinary acts of penance, without having ever done anything to deserve them. She has the same number of maids of honour, whom she suffers to go in colours, but she herself never quits mourning, and sure nothing can be more dismal than mournings here, even for a brother. There is not the least bit of linen to be seen; all black crepe instead of it; the neck, ears and side of the face covered with a plaited piece of the same stuff and the face that peeps out in the midst of it looks as if it were pilloried. The widows wear over and above, a crepe forehead-cloth, and in this solemn weed go to all the public places of diversion without scruple.

The next day I was to wait on the Empress Amelia, who is now at her palace of retirement, half a mile from the town. I had there the pleasure of seeing a diversion wholly new to me, but which is the common amusement of this court. The Empress herself was seated on a little throne at the end of the fine alley in the garden, and on each side of her ranged two parties of her ladies of honour with other young ladies of quality headed by the two young Archduchesses, all dressed in their hair, full of jewels, with fine light guns in their hands, and at proper distances were placed three oval pictures which were the marks to be shot at. The first was that of a cupid filling a bumper of Burgundy, and the motto, ''Tis easy to be valiant here'; the second a fortune holding a garland in her hand, the motto 'For her whom Fortune favours'. The third was a sword with a laurel wreath on the point, the motto 'Here is no shame to the vanquished'. Near the Empress was a gilded trophy wreathed with flowers and made of little crooks, on which were hung rich Turkish handkerchiefs, tippets, ribbons, laces etc. for the small prizes. The Empress gave the first with her own hand, which was a fine ruby ring set round with diamonds, in a gold snuff box. There was for the second a little cupid set with brilliants and besides these a set of fine china for a tea table, encased in gold, japan trunks, fans, and many gallantries of the same nature. All the men of quality at Vienna were spectators, but only the ladies had permission to shoot, and the Archduchess Amelia carried off the first prize. I was very well pleased with having seen this entertainment, and I don't know but it might make as good a figure as the prize shooting in the Aeneid, if I could write as well as Virgil. This is the favourite pleasure of the Emperor, and there is rarely a week without some feast of this kind, which makes the young ladies skilful enough to defend a fort and they laughed very much to see me afraid to handle a gun.

My dear sister, you will easily pardon an abrupt conclusion. I believe by this time you are ready to fear I would never conclude at all.

Vienna, 1 October 1716

To the Lady X—,

You desire me, madam, to send you some account of the customs here, and at the same time a description of Vienna. I am always willing to obey your commands, but I must upon this occasion desire you to take the will for the deed. If I should undertake to tell you all the particulars in which the manner here differ from ours, I must write a whole quire of the dullest stuff that ever was read, or printed without being read.

Their dress agrees with the French or English in no one article but wearing petticoats. They have many fashions peculiar to themselves; as that 'tis indecent for a widow ever to wear green or rose colour, but all the other gayest colours at her own discretion. The asemblies here are the only regular diversion, the operas being always at court and commonly on some particular occasion. Madam Rabutin has the assembly constantly every night at her house, and the other ladies, whenever they have a fancy to display the magnificence of their apartments, or oblige a friend by complimenting them on the day of their saint, they declare that on such a day the assembly shall be at their house in honour of the feast of the count or countess such-a-one. These days are called days of gala, and all the friends or relations of the lady whose saint it is are obliged to appear in their best clothes, and all their jewels. The mistress of the house takes no particular notice of anybody, nor returns anybody's visit; and, whoever pleases may go without the formality of being presented. The company are entertained with ice in several forms, winter and summer; afterwards they divide into several parties of ombre, piquet or conversation, all games of hazard being forbid. I saw the other day the gala for Count Althann, the Emperor's favourite, and never in my life saw so many fine clothes ill-fancied. They embroider the richest gold stuffs and provided they can make their clothes expensive enough that is all the taste they show in them. On other days, the general dress is a scarf and what you please under it.

But now I am speaking of Vienna, I am sure you expect I should say something of the convents; they are of all sorts and sizes, but I am best pleased with that of St Lawrence, where the ease and neatness they seem to live with appears to be much more edifying than those stricter orders where perpetual penance and nastiness must breed discontent and wretchedness. The nuns are all of quality. I think there is to the number of fifty. They have each of them a little cell perfectly clean, the walls covered with pictures more or less fine, according to their quality. A long white stone gallery runs by all of them, furnished with the pictures of exemplary sisters; the chapel extreme neat and richly adorned. But I could not forbear laughing at their showing me a wooden head of our Saviour, which they assured me spoke during the Siege of Vienna; and as a proof of it, bid me mark his mouth, which had been open ever since. Nothing can be more becoming than the dress of these nuns. It is a fine white camlet, the sleeves turned up with fine white calico, and their headdress of the same, only a small veil of black crepe that falls behind. They have a lower sort of serving nuns that wait on them as their chambermaids. They receive all visits of women and play at ombre in their chambers with permission of the abbess, which is very easy to be obtained. I never saw an old woman so good-natured; she is near fourscore and yet shows very little sign of decay, being still lively and cheerful. She caressed me as if I had been her daughter, giving me some pretty things of her own work and sweetmeats in abundance. The grate is not one of the most rigid; it is not very hard to put a head through, and I don't doubt but a man, a little more slender than ordinary, might squeeze in his whole person. The young Count of Salm came to the grate while I was there and the abbess gave him her hand to kiss.

But I was surprised to find here the only beautiful young woman I have seen at Vienna and not only beautiful but genteel, witty and agreeable, of a great family and who had been the admiration of the town. I could not forbear showing my surprise at seeing a nun like her. She made me a thousand obliging compliments and desired me to come often. It will be an infinite pleasure to me, said she sighing, to see you but I avoid with the greatest care seeing any of my former acquaintance, and whenever they come to our convent I lock myself in my cell. I observed tears come into her eyes, which touched me extremely, and I began to talk to her in that strain of tender pity she inspired me with; but she would not own to me that she is not perfectly happy. I have since endeavoured to learn the real cause of her retirement, without being able to get any account, but that everybody was surprised at it, and nobody guessed the reason. I have been several times to see her, but it gives me too much melancholy to see so agreeable a young creature buried alive and I am not surprised that nuns have so often inspired violent passions; the pity one naturally feels for them, when they seem worthy of another destiny, making an easy way for yet more tender sentiments and I never in my life had so little charity for the Roman Catholic religion as since I see the misery it occasions so many poor unhappy women! And the gross superstition of the common people, who are some or other of them, day and night offering bits of candle to the wooden figures that are set up almost in every street. The processions I see very often are a pageantry as offensive and apparently contradictory to all common sense as the pagodas of China. God knows whether it be the womanly spirit of contradiction that works in me, but there never before was such zeal against popery in the heart of, dear madam, etc.

Vienna, 16 January 1717

To Lady Mar,

I am now, dear sister, to take leave of you for a long time, and of Vienna for ever, designing tomorrow to begin my journey through Hungary, in spite of the excessive cold and deep snows, which are enough to damp a greater courage than I am mistress of, but my principle of passive obedience carries me through everything. I have had my audiences of leave of the Empresses. His imperial majesty was pleased to be present when I waited on the reigning empress and after a very obliging conversation both their imperial majesties invited me to take Vienna in my road back, but I have no thoughts of enduring over again so great a fatigue.

I delivered a letter to the Empress from the Duchess of Blankenburg. I stayed but a few days at that court, though her highness pressed me very much to stay, and when I left her, engaged me to write to her. I writ you a long letter from thence, which I hope you have received, though you don't mention it; but I believe I forgot to tell you one curiosity in all the German courts which I cannot forbear taking notice of. All the princes keep favourite dwarfs. The Emperor and Empress have two of these little monsters, as ugly as devils, especially the female, but all bedaubed with diamonds and stands at her majesty's elbow in all public places. The Duke of Wolfenbüttel has one, and the Duchess of Blankenburg is not without hers, but indeed the most proportionable I ever saw. I am told the King of Denmark has so far improved upon this fashion that his dwarf is his chief minister. I can assign no reason for their fondness for these pieces of deformity, but the opinion that all the absolute princes have, that it is below them to converse with the rest of mankind, and not to be quite alone they are forced to seek their companions amongst the refuse of human nature, these creatures being the only part of their court privileged to talk freely to them.

I am at present confined to my chamber by a sore throat, and am really glad of the excuse to avoid seeing people that I love well enough to be very much mortified when I think I am going to part with them for ever. 'Tis true, the Austrians are not commonly the most polite people in the world nor the most agreeable, but Vienna is inhabited by all nations, and I had formed to myself a little society of such as were perfectly to my own taste. And though the number was not very great, I could never pick up in any other place such a number of reasonable, agreeable people. We were almost always together, and you know I have ever been of opinion that a chosen conversation, composed of a few that one esteems, is the greatest happiness of life. Here are some Spaniards of both sexes that have all the vivacity and generosity of sentiments anciently ascribed to their nation, and could I believe that the whole kingdom were like them, I should wish nothing more than to end my days there.

The ladies of my acquaintance have so much goodness for me, they cry whenever they see me since I have determined to undertake this journey; and, indeed, I am not very easy when I reflect on what I am going to suffer. Almost everybody I see frights me with some new difficulty. Prince Eugene has been so good as to say all the things he could to persuade me to stay till the Danube is thawed, that I may have the convenience of going by water, assuring me that the houses in Hungary are such as are no defence against the weather, and that I shall be obliged to travel three or four days between Buda and Essek without finding any house at all, through desert plains covered with snow, where the cold is so violent many have been killed by it. I own these terrors have made a very deep impression on my mind, because I believe he tells me things truly as they are, and nobody can be better informed of them.

Now I have named that great man, I am sure you expect I should say something particular of him, having the advantage of seeing him very often, but I am as unwilling to speak of him at Vienna as I should be to talk of Hercules in the court of Omphale, if I had seen him there. I don't know what comfort other people find in considering the weaknesses of great men because, it brings them nearer to their own level but 'tis always a mortification to me to observe that there is no perfection in humanity. The young Prince of Portugal is the admiration of the whole court. He is handsome and polite, with a great vivacity. All the officers tell wonders of his gallantry in the last campaign. He is lodged at court with all the honours due to his rank.

Adieu, dear sister; this is the last account you will have from me of Vienna. If I survive my journey you shall hear from me again. I can say with great truth, in the words of Moneses, I have long learnt to hold myself as nothing, but when I think of the fatigue my poor infant must suffer, I have all a mother's fondness in my eyes, and all her tender passions in my heart.

P.S. I have writ a letter to my Lady—that I believe she won't like, and upon cooler reflection I think I had done better to have let it alone, but I was downright peevish at all her questions, and her ridiculous imagination, that I have certainly seen abundance of wonders which I keep to myself out of mere malice. She is angry that I won't lie like other travellers. I verily believe she expects I should tell her of the anthropophagi, and men whose heads grow below their shoulders. However, pray say something to pacify her.

Vienna, 16 January 1717

To Alexander Pope,
I have not time to answer your letter, being in all the hurry of preparing for my journey, but I think I ought to bid adieu to my friends with the same solemnity as if I was going to mount a breach, at least, if I am to believe the information of the people here, who denounce all sort of terrors to me; and indeed the weather is at present such as very few ever set out in.

I am threatened at the same time with being froze to death, buried in the snow and taken by the Tartars, who ravage that part of Hungary I am to pass. 'Tis true we shall have a considerable escort so that possibly I may be diverted with a new scene by finding myself in the midst of a battle. How my adventures will conclude I leave entirely to Providence; if comically, you shall hear of them.

Pray be so good as to tell Mr—I have received his letter. Make him my adieus; if I live I will answer it. The same compliment to my Lady Rich.

Peterwardein, 30 January 1717

To Lady Mar,

At length, dear sister, I am safely arrived, with all my family in good health, at Peterwardein [Novi Sad], having suffered little from the rigour of the season (against which we were well provided by furs) and found everywhere, by the care of sending before, such tolerable accommodation that I can hardly forbear laughing when I recollect all the frightful ideas that were given me of this journey, which were wholly owing to the tenderness of my Vienna friends and their desire of keeping me with them for this winter. Perhaps it will not be disagreeable to give you a short journal of my journey, being through a country entirely unknown to you, and very little passed even by the Hungarians themselves, who generally choose to take the convenience of going down the Danube. We have had the blessing of being favoured with finer weather than is common at this time of the year, though the snow was so deep we were obliged to have our coaches fixed upon traineaus, which move so swift and so easily 'tis by far the most agreeable manner of travelling post.

We came to Raab [. . .] the second day from Vienna, on the seventeenth instant, where Mr Wortley sending word of our arrival to the governor, we had the best house in the town provided for us, the garrison put under arms, a guard ordered at our door and all other honours paid to us; the governor and all other officers immediately waiting on Mr Wortley to know if there was anything to be done for his service. The Bishop of Temeswar came to visit us, with great civility, earnestly pressing us to dine with him the next day, which, we refusing, as being resolved to pursue our journey, he sent us several baskets of winter fruit, and a great variety of Hungarian wines with a young hind just killed. This is a prelate of great power in this country, of the ancient family of Nádasdy so considerable for many ages in this kingdom. He is a very polite, agreeable, cheerful old man, wearing the Hungarian habit with a venerable white beard down to his girdle.

Raab is a strong town, well garrisoned and fortified, and was a long time the frontier town between the Turkish and German empires. It has its name from the river Raab on which it is situated, just on its meeting with the Danube, in an open champaign country. It was first taken by the Turks under the command of the Pasha Sinan in the reign of Sultan Amurath III, in the year 1594. The governor being supposed to have betrayed it, was afterwards beheaded by the emperor's command. The counts of Schwarzenberg and Palffy retook it by surprise, 1598, since which time it has remained in the hands of the Germans, though the Turks once more attempted to gain it by stratagem, 1642. The cathedral is large and well built, which is all that I saw remarkable in the town.

Leaving Comora [. . .] on the other side the river we went the eighteenth to Nosmuhl, a small village where however, we made shift to find tolerable accommodation. We continued two days travelling between this place and Buda, through the finest plains in the world, as even as if they were paved, and extreme fruitful, but for the most part desert and uncultivated, laid waste by the long war between the Turk and the Emperor, and the more cruel civil war occasioned by the barbarous persecution of the Protestant religion by the Emperor Leopold. That prince has left behind him the character of an extraordinary piety, and was naturally of a mild merciful temper; but, putting his conscience into the hands of a Jesuit, he was more cruel and treacherous to his poor Hungarian subjects than ever the Turk has been to the Christians, breaking without scruple his coronation oath and his faith, solemnly given in many public treaties. Indeed, nothing can be more melancholy than travelling through Hungary, reflecting on the former flourishing state of that kingdom, and seeing such a noble spot of earth almost uninhabited.

This is also the present circumstances of Buda, where we arrived very early the twenty second, once the royal seat of the Hungarian kings, where their palace was reckoned one of the most beautiful buildings of the age, now wholly destroyed, no part of the town having been repaired since the last siege but the fortifications and the castle, which is the present residence of the governor, General Regal, an officer of great merit. He came immediately to see us, and carried us in his coach to his house, where I was received by his lady with all possible civility, and magnificently entertained. This city is situate upon a little hill on the south side of the Danube, the castle being much higher than the town, from whence the prospect is very noble. Without the walls lie a vast number of little houses, or rather huts, that they call the Rascian town, being altogether inhabited by that people. The governor assured me it would furnish 12,000 fighting men. These towns look very odd; their houses stand in rows, many thousands of them so close together that they appear at a little distance like old fashioned thatched tents. They consist, every one of them, of one hovel above and another underground; these are their summer and winter apartments.

Buda was first taken by Süleiman the Magnificent in 1526, and lost the following year to Ferdinand I, King of Bohemia. Süleiman regained it, 1529, by the treachery of the garrison, and voluntarily gave it into the hand of King John of Hungary, after whose death, his son being an infant, Ferdinand laid siege to it and the Queen Mother was forced to call Süleiman to her aid, who raised the siege, but left a Turkish garrison in the town and commanded her to remove her court from thence, which she was forced to submit to in 1541.

It resisted afterwards the sieges laid to it by the Marquis of Brandenburg, 1542; Count Schwarzenberg, 1598, General Russworm in 1602, and the Duke of Lorrain, commander of the emperor's forces, in 1684, to whom it yielded, 1686, after an obstinate defence, Abdul Pasha, the governor, being killed fighting in the breach with a Roman bravery. The loss of this town was so important, and so much resented by the Turks, that it occasioned the deposing of their Emperor Mehmed IV, the year following.

We did not proceed on our journey till the twenty third, passing through Adom and Fodwar, both considerable towns when in the hands of the Turks. They are now quite ruined; only the remains of some Turkish towers show something of what they have been. This part of the country is very much overgrown with wood and so little frequented 'tis incredible what vast numbers of wildfowl we saw, who often live here to a good old age, and, undisturbed by guns, in quiet sleep.

We came the twenty fifth to Mohács, and were showed the field near it where Louis, the young King of Hungary, lost his army and his life, being drowned in a ditch trying to fly from Balybeus, the general of Süleiman the Magnificent. This battle opened the first passage for the Turks into the heart of Hungary. I don't name to you the little villages, of which I can say nothing remarkable, but I'll assure you, I have always found a warm stove and great plenty, particularly of wild boar, venison and all kinds of *gibier*. The few people that inhabit Hungary live easily enough. They have no money, but the woods and plains afford them provision in great abundance. They were ordered to give us all things necessary, even what horses we pleased to demand, gratis, but Mr Wortley would not oppress the poor country people by making use of this order, and always paid them to the full worth of what we had from them. They were so surprised at this unexpected generosity, which they are very little used to, they always pressed upon us at parting, a dozen of fat pheasants, or something of that sort, for a present. Their dress is very primitive, being only a plain sheep's skin without other dressing than being dried in the sun and a cap and boots of the same stuff. You may imagine this lasts them many winters, and thus they have very little occasion for money.

The twenty sixth we passed over the frozen Danube with all our equipage and carriages. We met on the other side General Veterani, who invited us with great civility to pass the night at a little castle of his a few miles off, assuring us we should have a very hard day's journey to reach Essek [. . .], which we found but too true, the woods being scarce passable and very dangerous, from the vast quantity of wolves that herd in them. We came, however, safe, though late, to Essek, where we stayed a day to despatch a courier with letters to the Pasha of Belgrade, and I took that opportunity of seeing the town, which is not very large, but fair built and well fortified. This was a town of great trade, very rich and populous when in the hands of the Turks. It is situated on the Drave, which runs into the Danube. The bridge was esteemed one of the most extraordinary in the world, being 8000 paces long, and all built of oak, which was burnt, and the city laid in ashes by Count Leslie, 1685, but was again repaired and fortified by the Turks who, however, abandoned it, 1687, and General Dünnewalt took possession of it for the Emperor, in whose hands it has remained ever since, and is esteemed one of the bulwarks of Hungary. The twenty eighth we went to Bocowar, a very large Rascian town, all built after the manner I have described to you. We were met out there by Colonel—, who would not suffer us to go anywhere but to his quarters, where I found his wife a very agreeable Hungarian lady, and his niece and daughter, two pretty young women, crowded into three or four Rascian houses cast into one and made as neat and convenient as those places were capable of being made. The Hungarian ladies are much hand-somer than those of Austria. All the Vienna beauties are of that country; they are generally very fair and well-shaped. Their dress I think extreme becoming. This lady was in a gown of scarlet velvet, lined and faced with sables, made exact to her shape, and the skirt falling to her feet. The sleeves are strait to their arms and the stays buttoned before, with two rows of little buttons of gold, pearl or diamonds. On their heads they wear a cap embroidered with a tassel of gold that hangs low on one side, lined with sable, or some other fine fur. They gave us a handsome dinner, and I thought their conversation very polite and agreeable. They would accompany us part of our way.

The twenty ninth we arrived here, where we were met by the commandant at the head of all the officers of the garrison. We are lodged in the best apartment of the governor's house, and entertained in a very splendid manner by the emperor's order. We wait here till all points are adjusted concerning our reception on the Turkish frontiers. Mr Wortley's courier, which he sent from Essek, returned this morning with the Pasha's answer in a purse of scarlet satin, which the interpreter here has translated. 'Tis to promise him to be honourably received, and desires him to appoint where he would be met by the Turkish convoy. He has despatched the courier back, naming Betsko, a village in the mid-way between Peterwardein and Belgrade. We shall stay here till we receive the answer.

Thus, dear sister, I have given you a very particular and, I am afraid you'll think, a tedious account of this part of my travels. It was not an affectation of showing my reading that has made me tell you some little scraps of the history of the towns I have passed through. I have always avoided anything of that kind, when I spoke of places that I believe you knew the story of as well as myself, but Hungary being a part of the world which I believe quite new to you, I thought you might read with some pleasure an account of it, which I have been very solicitous to get from the best hands. However, if you don't like it, 'tis in your power to forbear reading it. I am, dear sister, etc.

I am promised to have this letter carefully sent to Vienna.

Belgrade, 12 February 1717

To Alexander Pope,

I did verily intend to write you a long letter from Peterwardein, where I expected to stay three or four days, but the Pasha here was in such haste to see us that he despatched our courier back which Mr Wortley had sent to know the time he would send the convoy to meet us, without suffering him to pull off his boots. My letters were not thought important enough to stop our journey and we left Peterwardein the next day, being waited on by the chief officers of the garrison and a considerable convoy of Germans and Rascians. The Emperor has several regiments of these people, but to say truth, they are rather plunderers than soldiers, having no pay and being obliged to furnish their own arms and horses. They rather look like vagabond gypsies or stout beggars than regular troops. I can't forbear speaking a word of this race of creatures who are very numerous all over Hungary. They have a patriarch of their own at Grand Cairo, and are really of the Greek church, but their extreme ignorance gives their priests occasion to impose several new notions upon them. These fellows letting their hair and beards grow inviolate, make exactly the figure of the Indian Brahmins. They are heirs-general to all the money of the laity for which, in return, they give them formal passports signed and sealed for heaven, and the wives and children only inherit the houses and cattle. In most other points they follow the Greek rites.

This little digression has interrupted my telling you we passed over the fields of Karlowitz, where the last great victory was obtained by Prince Eugene over the Turks. The marks of that glorious bloody day are yet recent, the field being strewed with the skulls and carcases of unburied men, horses and camels. I could not look without horror on such numbers of mangled human bodies, and reflect on the injustice of war that makes murder not only necessary but meritorious. Nothing seems to me a plainer proof of the irrationality of mankind, whatever fine claims we pretend to reason, than the rage with which they contest for a small spot of ground, when such vast parts of fruitful earth lie quite uninhabited. 'Tis true, custom has now made it unavoidable, but can there be a greater demonstration of want of reason than a custom being firmly established so plainly contrary to the interest of man in general? I am a good deal inclined to believe Mr Hobbes that the state of nature is a state of war, but thence I conclude human nature not rational, if the word reason means common sense, as I suppose it does. I have a great many admirable arguments to support this reflection but I won't trouble you with them, but return in a plain style to the history of my travels.

We were met at Betsko, a village in the midway between Belgrade and Peterwardein, by an aga of the janissaries, with a body of Turks, exceeding the Germans by one hundred men, though the Pasha had engaged to send exactly the same number. You may judge by this of their fears. I am really persuaded that they hardly thought the odds of one hundred men set them even with the Germans. However, I was very uneasy till they were parted, fearing some quarrel might arise, notwithstanding the parole given.

We came late to Belgrade, the deep snows making the ascent to it very difficult. It seems a strong city, fortified on the east side by the Danube and on the south by the river Save, and was formerly the barrier of Hungary. It was first taken by Süleiman the Magnificent and since, by the Emperor's forces, led by the Elector of Bavaria, who held it only two year, it being retaken by the Grand Vizier and is now fortified with the utmost care and skill the Turks are capable of, and strengthened by a very numerous garrison of their bravest janissaries, commanded by a pasha seraskier (i.e. general). This last expression is not very just, for to say truth, the seraskier is commanded by the janissaries who have an absolute authority here, not much unlike a rebellion which you may judge of by the following story which at the same time, will give you an idea of the admirable intelligence of the governor of Peterwardein, though so few hours distant.

We were told by him at Peterwardein that the garrison and inhabitants of Belgrade were so weary of the war they had killed their pasha about two months ago in a mutiny, because he had suffered himself to be prevailed upon by a bribe of five purses (five hundred pounds sterling) to give permission to the Tartars to ravage the German frontiers. We were very well pleased to hear of such favourable dispositions in the people, but when we came hither we found the governor had been ill informed, and this is the real truth of the story.

The late pasha fell under the displeasure of his soldiers for no other reason but restraining their incursions on the Germans. They took it into their heads, from that mildness, that he was of intelligence with the enemy, and sent such information to the Grand Signor at Adrianople [Edirne]; but redress not coming quick enough from thence, they assembled themselves in a tumultuous manner, and by force dragged their pasha before the cadi and mufti, and there demanded justice in a mutinous way, one crying out why he protected the infidels? Another, why he squeezed them of their money? That easily guessing their purpose, he calmly replied to them that they asked him too many questions; he had but one life, which must answer for all. They immediately fell upon him with their scimitars, without waiting the sentence of their heads of the law, and in a few moments cut him in pieces. The present pasha has not dared to punish the murder; on the contrary, he affected to applaud the actors of it as brave fellows that knew how to do themselves justice. He takes all pretences of throwing money amongst the garrison, and suffers them to make little excursions into Hungary, where they burn some poor Rascian houses. You may imagine I cannot be very easy in a town which is really under the government of an insolent soldiery. We expected to be immediately dismissed after a night's lodging here, but the pasha detains us till he receives orders from Adrianople, which may possibly be a month a-coming.

In the meantime, we are lodged in one of the best houses, belonging to a very considerable man amongst them, and have a whole chamber of janissaries to guard us. My only diversion is the conversations of our host, Achmed Bey, a title something like that of count in Germany. His father was a great pasha, and he has been educated in the most polite eastern learning, being perfectly skilled in the Arabic and Persian languages, and is an extraordinary scribe, which they call *effendi*. This accomplishment makes way to the greatest preferments, but he has had the good sense to prefer an easy, quiet, secure life to all the dangerous honours of the Porte. He sups with us every night, and drinks wine very freely. You cannot imagine how much he is delighted with the liberty of conversing with me. He has explained to me many pieces of Arabian poetry which, I observed, are in numbers not unlike ours, generally alternate verse, and of a very musical sound. Their expressions of love are very passionate and lively. I am so much pleased with them, I really believe I should learn to read Arabic, if I was to stay here a few months. He has a very good library of their books of all kinds and, as he tells me, spends the greatest part of his life there. I pass for a great scholar with him, by relating to him some of the Persian tales, which I find are genuine. At first he believed I understood Persian. I have frequent disputes with him concerning the difference of our customs, particularly the confinements of women. He assures me, there is nothing at all in it; only, says he, we have the advantage that when our wives cheat us nobody knows it. He has wit, and is more polite than many Christian men of quality. I am very much entertained with him. He has had the curiosity to make one of our servants set him an alphabet of our letters, and can already write a good Roman hand. But these amusements do not hinder my wishing heartily to be out of this place, though the weather is colder than I believe it ever was anywhere but in Greenland. We have a very large stove constantly kept hot, and yet the windows of the room are frozen on the inside.

God knows when I may have an opportunity of sending this letter, but I have written it for the discharge of my own conscience, and you cannot now reproach me that one of yours makes ten of mine.

Adrianople, 1 April 1717

To Her Royal Highness the Princess of Wales,
I have now, madam, passed a journey that has not been undertaken by any Christian since the time of the Greek emperors, and I shall not regret all the fatigues I have suffered in it if it gives me an opportunity of amusing your Royal Highness by an account of places utterly unknown amongst us, the emperor's ambassadors and those few English that have come hither always going on the Danube to Nicopolis. But that river was now frozen, and Mr Wortley so zealous for the service of his majesty he would not defer his journey to wait for the convenience of that passage. We crossed the deserts of Serbia, almost quite overgrown with wood, though a country naturally fertile and the inhabitants industrious. But the oppression of the peasants is

so great, they are forced to abandon their houses and neglect their tillage, all they have being a prey to the janissaries, whenever they please to seize upon it. We had a guard of 500 of them, and I was almost in tears every day to see their insolencies in the poor villages through which we passed.

After seven days travelling through thick woods we came to Nissa [Niš], once the capital of Serbia, situate in a fine plain on the river Nissava, in a very good air and so fruitful a soil that the great plenty is hardly credible. I was certainly assured that the quantity of wine last vintage was so prodigious they were forced to dig holes in the earth to put it in, not having vessels enough in the town to hold it. The happiness of this plenty is scarce perceived by the oppressed people. I saw here a new occasion for my compassion. The wretches that had provided twenty waggons for our baggage from Belgrade hither for a certain hire, being all sent back without payment, some of their horses lamed and others killed, without any satisfaction made for them. The poor fellows came round the house weeping and tearing their hair and beards in the most pitiful manner, without getting anything but drubs from the insolent soldiers. I cannot express to your Royal Highness how much I was moved at this scene. I would have paid them the money out of my own pocket, with all my heart, but it would only have been giving so much to the aga who would have taken it from them without remorse.

After four days journey from this place over the mountains we came to Sofia, situated in a large beautiful plain on the river Isca, and surrounded with distant mountains. 'Tis hardly possible to see a more agreeable landscape. The city itself is very large and extremely populous. Here are hot baths, very famous for their medicinal virtues. Four days' journey from hence we arrived at Philippopolis [Plovdiv], after having passed the ridges between the mountains of Haemus and Rhodophe, which are always covered with snow. This town is situated on a rising ground near the river Hebrus and is almost wholly inhabited by Greeks. Here are still some ancient Christian churches. They have a bishop and several of the richest Greeks live here, but they are forced to conceal their wealth with great care, the appearance of poverty, which includes part of its inconveniences, being all their security against feeling it in earnest. The country from hence to Adrianople is the finest in the world. Vines grow wild on all the hills and the perpetual spring they enjoy makes everything look gay and flourishing. But this climate, as happy as it seems, can never be preferred to England with all its snows and frosts, while we are blessed with an easy government under a king who makes his own happiness consist in the liberty of his people and chooses rather to be looked upon as their father than their master.

This theme would carry me very far and I am sensible I have already tired out your Royal Highness' patience, but my letter is in your hands and you may make it as short as you please by throwing it into the fire when you are weary of reading it.

I am, madam, with the greatest respect etc.

Adrianople, 1 April 1717

To Lady—,
I am now got into a new world, where everything I see appears to me a change of scene, and I write to your ladyship with some content of mind, hoping at least that you will find the charm of novelty in my letters, and no longer reproach me that I tell you nothing extraordinary. I won't trouble you with a relation of our tedious journey, but I must not omit what I saw remarkable at Sofia, one of the most beautiful towns in the Turkish empire, and famous for its hot baths, that are resorted to both for diversion and health. I stopped here one day on purpose to see them. Designing to go incognito I hired a Turkish coach. These voitures are not at all like ours, but much more convenient for the country, the heat being so great that glasses would be very troublesome. They are made a good deal in the manner of the Dutch coaches, having wooden lattices painted and gilded, the inside being also painted with baskets and nosegays of flowers, intermixed commonly with little poetical mottos. They are covered all over with scarlet cloth, lined with silk, and very often richly embroidered and fringed. This covering entirely hides the persons in them, but may be thrown back at pleasure and the ladies peep through the lattices. They hold four people very conveniently, seated on cushions, but not raised.

In one of these covered waggons, I went to the bagnio about ten o'clock. It was already full of women.

It is built of stone in the shape of a dome, with no windows but in the roof, which gives light enough. There was five of these domes joined together, the outmost being less than the rest and serving only as a hall, where the portress stood at the door. Ladies of quality generally give this woman the value of a crown or ten shillings and I did not forget that ceremony. The next room is a very large one paved with marble, and all round it raised two sofas of marble one above another. There were four fountains of cold water in this room, falling first into marble basins, and then running on the floor in little channels made for that purpose, which carried the streams into the next room, something less than this, with the same sort of marble sofas, but so hot with steams of sulphur proceeding from the baths joining to it, 'twas impossible to stay there with one's clothes on. The two other domes were the hot baths, one of which had cocks of cold water turning into it to temper it to what degree of warmth the bathers have a mind to.

I was in my travelling habit, which is a riding dress, and certainly appeared very extraordinary to them. Yet there was not one of them that showed the least surprise or impertinent curiosity, but received me with all the obliging civility possible. I know no European court where the ladies would have behaved themselves in so polite a manner to a stranger. I believe, in the whole, there were two hundred women, and yet none of those disdainful smiles or satirical whispers that never fail in our assemblies when anybody appears that is not dressed exactly in fashion. They repeated over and over to me; 'Güzelle, pek güzelle', which is nothing but 'charming, very charming'. The first sofas were covered with cushions and rich carpets, on which sat the ladies, and on the second their slaves behind them, but without any distinction of rank by their dress, all being in the state of nature, that is, in plain English, stark naked, without any beauty or defect concealed. Yet there was not the least wanton smile or immodest gesture amongst them. They walked and moved with the same majestic grace which Milton describes of our general mother. There were many amongst them as exactly proportioned as ever any goddess was drawn by the pencil of Guido or Titian, and most of their skins shiningly white, only adorned by their beautiful hair divided into many tresses, hanging on their shoulders, braided either with pearl or ribbon, perfectly representing the figures of the Graces.

I was here convinced of the truth of a reflection I had often made, that if it was the fashion to go naked, the face would be hardly observed. I perceived that the ladies with finest skins and most delicate shapes had the greatest share of my admiration, though their faces were sometimes less beautiful than those of their companions. To tell you the truth, I had wickedness enough to wish secretly that Mr Gervase [a portrait painter] could have been there invisible. I fancy it would have very much improved his art to see so many fine women naked, in different postures, some in conversation, some working, others drinking coffee or sherbet, and many negligently lying on their cushions while their slaves (generally pretty girls of seventeen or eighteen) were employed in braiding their hair in several pretty manners. In short, 'tis the women's coffee house, where all the news of the town is told, scandal invented etc. They generally take this diversion once a week, and stay there at least four or five hours, without getting cold by immediate coming out of the hot bath into the cool room, which was very surprising to me. The lady that seemed the most considerable amongst them entreated me to sit by her and would fain have undressed me for the bath. I excused myself with some difficulty, they being however all so earnest in persuading me, I was at last forced to open my shirt, and show them my stays, which satisfied them very well, for I saw they believed I was so locked up in that machine, that it was not in my own power to open it, which contrivance they attributed to my husband. I was charmed with their civility and beauty, and should have been very glad to pass more time with them, but Mr Wortley resolving to pursue his journey the next morning early I was in haste to see the ruins of Justinian's church, which did not afford me so agreeable a prospect as I had left, being little more than a heap of stones.

Adieu, madam, I am sure I have now entertained you with an account of such a sight as you never saw in your life, and what no book of travels could inform you of, as 'tis no less than death for a man to be found in one of these places.

Adrianople, 1 April 1717

To Lady Bristol,
As I never can forget the smallest of your ladyship's
commands, my first business here has been to enquire
after the stuffs you ordered me to look for, without
being able to find what you would like. The difference
of the dress here and at London is so great, the same
sort of things are not proper for caftans and manteaus.
However, I will not give over my search but renew
it again at Constantinople, though I have reason to
believe there is nothing finer than what is to be found
here, being at present the residence of the court.

The Grand Signor's eldest daughter was married
some few days before I came and upon that occasion
the Turkish ladies display all their magnificence. The
bride was conducted to her husband's house in very
great splendour. She is widow of the late Vizier, who
was killed at Peterwardein, though that ought rather
to be called a contract than a marriage, not ever having
lived with him. However, the greatest part of his wealth
is hers. He had the permission of visiting her in the
seraglio, and, being one of the handsomest men in the
Empire, had very much engaged her affections. When
she saw this second husband, who is at least fifty, she
could not forbear bursting into tears. He is a man of
merit, and the declared favourite of the Sultan (which
they call *musahib*) but that is not enough to make him
pleasing in the eyes of a girl of thirteen.

The government here is entirely in the hands of the

army and the Grand Signor with all his absolute power as much a slave as any of his subjects, and trembles at a janissary's frown. Here is indeed a much greater appearance of subjection than amongst us. A minister of state is not spoke to but upon the knee; should a reflection on his conduct be dropped in a coffee house (for they have spies everywhere) the house would be razed to the ground, and perhaps the whole company put to the torture. No huzzaing mobs, senseless pamphlets and tavern disputes about politics

A consequential ill that freedom draws;
A bad effect, but from a noble cause.

None of our harmless calling names! But when a minister here displeases the people in three hours time he is dragged even from his master's arms. They cut off his hands, head and feet, and throw them before the palace gate with all the respect in the world, while the Sultan (to whom they all profess an unlimited adoration) sits trembling in his apartment, and dare neither defend nor revenge his favourite. This is the blessed condition of the most absolute monarch upon earth, who owns no law but his will.

I cannot help wishing, in the loyalty of my heart, that the parliament would send hither a ship load of your passive obedient men, that they might see arbitrary government in its clearest, strongest light, where 'tis hard to judge whether the prince, people or ministers are most miserable. I could make many reflections on this subject but I know, madam, your own good sense has already furnished you with better than I am capable of.

I went yesterday with the French Ambassadress to see the Grand Signor in his passage to the mosque. He was preceded by a numerous guard of janissaries with vast white feathers on their heads, as also by the *sipahis* and *bostcis* (these are foot and horse guards) and the royal gardeners, which are a very considerable body of men, dressed in different habits of fine lively colours so that, at a distance, they appeared like a parterre of tulips. After them the Aga of the janissaries in a robe of purple velvet lined with silver tissue, his horse led by two slaves richly dressed. Next him the Kilar Aga (your ladyship knows this is the chief guardian of the seraglio ladies) in a deep yellow cloth (which suited very well to his black face) lined with sables and last his sublimity himself, in green lined with the fur of a black muscovite fox, which is supposed worth a thousand pounds sterling, mounted on a fine horse with furniture embroidered with jewels. Six more horses richly furnished were led after him and two of his principal courtiers bore one his gold and the other his silver coffee pot, on a staff. Another carried a silver stool on his head for him to sit on. It would be too tedious to tell your ladyship the various dresses and turbans by which their rank is distinguished, but they were all extremely rich and gay to the number of some thousands that, perhaps there cannot be seen a more beautiful procession. The Sultan appeared to us a handsome man of about forty, with a very graceful air but with something severe in his countenance, his eyes very full and black. He happened to stop under the window where we stood, and, I suppose being told who we were, looked upon us very attentively, that we had full leisure to consider him and the French Ambassadress agreed with me as to his good mien.

I see that lady very often; she is young and her conversation would be a great relief to me if I could persuade her to live without those forms and ceremonies that make life formal and tiresome. But she is so delighted with her guards, her twenty four footmen, gentlemen ushers, etc., that she would rather die than make me a visit without them, not to reckon a coachful of attending damsels y'cleped maids of honour. What vexes me is that as long as she will visit with this troublesome equipage I am obliged to do the same. However, our mutual interest makes us much together. I went with her the other day all round the town in an open gilt chariot, with our joint train of attendants, preceded by our guards, who might have summoned the people to see what they had never seen, nor ever would see again; two young Christian ambassadresses never yet having been in this country at the same time, nor I believe ever will again. Your ladyship may easily imagine that we drew a vast crowd of spectators, but all silent as death. If any of them had taken the liberties of our mob upon any strange sight our janissaries had made no scruple of falling on them with their scimitars, without danger for so doing, being above the law. Yet these people have some good qualities; they are very zealous and faithful where they serve, and look upon it as their business to fight for you on all occasions, of which I had a very pleasant instance in a village on this side Philippopolis, where we were met by our domestic guard. I happened to bespeak pigeons for my supper, upon which one of my janissaries went immediately to the cadi (the chief civil officer of the town) and ordered him to send in some dozens. The poor man answered that he had already sent about but could get none. My janissary, in the height of his zeal for my service immediately locked him up prisoner in his room, telling him he deserved death for his impudence in offering to excuse his not obeying my command but out of respect to me he would not punish him but by my order and accordingly came very gravely to me to ask what should be done to him adding, by way of compliment, that if I pleased he would bring me his head. This may give some idea of the unlimited power of these fellows, who are all sworn brothers, and bound to revenge the injuries done to one another, whether at Cairo, Aleppo or any part of the world and this inviolable league makes them so powerful the greatest man at court never speaks to them but in a flattering tone, and in Asia any man that is rich is forced to enrol himself a janissary to secure his estate. But I have already said enough and I dare swear, dear madam, that by this time, 'tis a very comfortable reflection to you that there is no possibility of your receiving such a tedious letter but once in six months. 'Tis that consideration has given me the assurance to entertain you so long and will, I hope, plead the excuse of, dear madam, etc.

Adrianople, 1 April 1717

To Lady Mar,
I wish to God, dear sister, that you were as regular in letting me have the pleasure of knowing what passes on your side of the globe as I am careful in endeavouring to amuse you by the account of all I see that I think you care to hear of. You content yourself with telling me over and over that the town is very dull. It may possibly be dull to you when every day does not present you with something new, but for me that am in arrear at least two months news, all that seems very stale with you would be fresh and sweet here. Pray let me into more particulars. I will try to awaken your gratitude by giving you a full and true relation of the novelties of this place, none of which would surprise you more than a sight of my person, as I am now in my Turkish habit, though I believe you would be of my opinion that 'tis admirably becoming. I intend to send you my picture. In the meantime accept of it here.

The first piece of my dress is a pair of drawers, very full, that reach to my shoes, and conceal the legs more modestly than your petticoats. They are of a thin rose colour damask, brocaded with silver flowers, my shoes of white kid leather embroidered with gold. Over this hangs my smock of a fine white silk gauze, edged with embroidery. This smock has wide sleeves hanging half way down the arm and is closed at the neck with a diamond button; but the shape and colour of the bosom is very well to be distinguished through it. The *entari* is a waistcoat made close to the shape, of white and gold damask with very long sleeves falling back and fringed with deep gold fringe, and should have diamond or pearl buttons. My caftan of the same stuff with my drawers, is a robe exactly fitted to my shape and reaching to my feet, with very long straight-falling sleeves. Over this is the girdle of about four fingers broad which all that can afford have entirely of diamonds or other precious stones; those that will not be at that expense have it of exquisite embroidery on satin, but it must be fastened before with a clasp of diamonds. The cüppe is a loose robe they throw off, or put on, according to the weather, being of a rich brocade (mine is green and gold) either lined with ermine or sables. The sleeves reach very little below the shoulders. The headdress is composed of a cap, called kalpak which is in winter of fine velvet embroidered with pearls or diamonds and in summer of a light shining silver stuff. This is fixed on one side of the head, hanging a little way down with a gold tassel, and bound on either with a circle of diamonds (as I have seen several) or a rich embroidered handkerchief. On the other side of the head the hair is laid flat and here the ladies are at liberty to show their fancies, some putting flowers, others a plume of heron's feathers and, in short, what they please; but the most general fashion is a large bouquet of jewels made like natural flowers; that is, the buds of pearl, the roses of different coloured rubies, the jessamines of diamonds, the jonquils of topazes, etc, so well set and enamelled 'tis hard to imagine anything of that kind so beautiful. The hair hangs at its full length behind, divided into tresses braided with pearl or ribbon, which is always in great quantity.

I never saw in my life so many fine heads of hair. I have counted a hundred and ten of these tresses of one lady, all natural. But, it must be owned that every beauty is more common here than with us. 'Tis surprising to see a young woman that is not very handsome. They have naturally the most beautiful complexions in the world and generally large black eyes. I can assure you with great truth that the court of England, though I believe it the fairest in Christendom, cannot show so many beauties as are under our protection here. They generally shape their eyebrows and both Greeks and Turks have a custom of putting round their eyes on the inside a black tincture that, at a distance, or by candlelight, adds very much to the blackness of them. I fancy many of our ladies would be overjoyed to know this secret, but 'tis too visible by day. They dye their nails rose colour; I own I cannot enough accustom myself to this fashion to find any beauty in it.

As to their morality or good conduct, I can say, like Harlequin, that 'tis just as 'tis with you, and the Turkish ladies don't commit one sin the less for not being Christians. Now that I am a little acquainted with their ways I cannot forbear admiring either the exemplary discretion or extreme stupidity of all the writers that have given accounts of them. 'Tis very easy to see they have more liberty than we have, no woman, of what rank so ever being permitted to go in the streets without two muslins, one that covers her face all but her eyes and another that hides the whole dress of her head, and hangs half way down her back and their shapes are also wholly concealed by a thing they call a *ferace* which no woman of any sort appears without. This has straight sleeves that reaches to their fingers ends and it laps all round them, not unlike a riding hood. In winter 'tis of cloth and in summer plain stuff or silk. You may guess then how effectually this disguises them, that there is no distinguishing the great lady from her slave and 'tis impossible for the most jealous husband to know his wife when he meets her, and no man dare either touch or follow a woman in the street.

This perpetual masquerade gives them entire liberty of following their inclinations without danger of discovery. The most usual method of intrigue is to send an appointment to the lover to meet the lady at a Jew's shop, which are as notoriously convenient as our Indian houses, and yet, even those that don't make use of them do not scruple to go to buy pennyworths and tumble over rich goods, which are chiefly to be found amongst that sort of people. The great ladies seldom let their gallants know who they are, and 'tis so difficult to find it out that they can very seldom guess at her name they have corresponded with above half a year together. You may easily imagine the number of faithful wives very small in a country where they have nothing to fear from their lovers' indiscretion, since we see so many that have the courage to expose themselves to that in this world, and all the threatened punishment of the next, which is never preached to the Turkish damsels. Neither have they much to apprehend from the resentment of their husbands, those ladies that are rich having all their money in their own hands, which they take with them upon a divorce with an addition which he is obliged to give them. Upon the whole, I look upon the Turkish women as the only free people in the empire. The very Divan [council] pays respect to them and the Grand Signor himself, when a pasha is executed, never violates the privileges of the harem (or women's apartment) which remains unsearched entire to the widow. They are queens of their slaves, which the husband has no permission so much as to look upon, except it be an old woman or two that his lady chooses. 'Tis true, their law permits them four wives, but there is no instance of a man of quality that makes use of this liberty, or of a woman of rank that would suffer it. When a husband happens to be inconstant, as those things will happen, he keeps his mistress in a house apart and visits her as privately as he can, just as 'tis with you. Amongst all the great men here, I only know the *tefterdar* (ie treasurer) that keeps a number of she-slaves for his own use (that is, on his own side of the house, for a slave once given to serve a lady is entirely at her disposal) and he is spoke of as a libertine, or what we should call a rake, and his wife won't see him, though she continues to live in his house.

Thus you see, dear sister, the manners of mankind do not differ so widely as our voyage writers would make us believe. Perhaps it would be more entertaining to add a few surprising customs of my own invention, but nothing seems to me so agreeable as truth, and I believe nothing so acceptable to you. I conclude with repeating the great truth of my being, dear sister etc.

Adrianople, 1 April 1718

To Sarah Chiswell,

In my opinion, dear Sarah I ought rather to quarrel with you for not answering my Nijmegen letter of August until December, than to excuse my not writing again till now. I am sure there is on my side a very good excuse for silence, having gone such tiresome land journeys, though I don't find the conclusion of them so bad as you seem to imagine. I am very easy here, and not in the solitude you fancy me. The great quantity of Greek, French, English and Italians that are under our protection, make their court to me from morning till night, and I'll assure you, are many of them very fine ladies, for there is no possibility for a Christian to live easily under this government but by the protection of an ambassador, and the richer they are, the greater the danger.

Those dreadful stories you have heard of the plague have very little foundation in truth. I own I have much ado to reconcile myself to the sound of a word which has always given me such terrible ideas, though I am convinced there is little more in it than in a fever, as a proof of which we passed through two or three towns most violently infected. In the very next house where we lay, in one of them, two persons died of it. Luckily for me I was so well deceived that I knew nothing of the matter and I was made believe that our second cook, who fell ill there had only a great cold. However, we left our doctor to take care of him, and yesterday they both arrived here in good health, and I am now let into the secret that he has had the plague. There are many that escape of it, neither is the air ever infected. I am persuaded it would be as easy to root it out here as out of Italy and France, but it does so little mischief they are not very solicitous about it, and are content to suffer this distemper, instead of our variety, which they are utterly unacquainted with.

A propos of distempers I am going to tell you a thing that I am sure will make you wish yourself here. The smallpox, so fatal and so general amongst us, is here entirely harmless by the invention of engrafting, which is the term they give it. There is a set of old women who make it their business to perform the operation. Every autumn in the month of September when the great heat is abated, people send one another to know if any of their family has a mind to have the smallpox. They make parties for this purpose and when they are met (commonly fifteen or sixteen together) the old woman comes with a nutshell full of the matter of the best sort of smallpox, and asks what veins you please to have opened. She immediately rips open that you offer to her with a large needle (which gives you no more pain than a common scratch) and puts into the vein as much venom as can lie upon the head of her needle, and after binds up the little wound with a hollow bit of shell, and in this manner opens four or five veins. The Grecians have commonly the superstition of opening one in the middle of the forehead, in each arm and on the breast to mark the sign of the cross, but this has a very ill effect, all these wounds leaving little scars, and is not done by those that are not super-stitious, who choose to have them in the legs or that part of the arm that is concealed. The children or young patients play together all the rest of the day, and are in perfect health until the eighth. Then the fever begins to seize them and they keep their beds two days, very seldom three. They have very rarely above twenty or thirty in their faces, which never mark, and in eight days time they are as well as before their illness. Where they are wounded there remains running sores during the distemper which I don't doubt is a great relief to it. Every year thousands undergo this operation, and the French Ambassador says pleasantly that they take the smallpox here by way of diversion, as they take the waters in other countries. There is no example of any one that has died in it, and you may believe I am well satisfied of the safety of the experiment, since I intend to try it on my dear little son. I am patriot enough to take pains to bring this useful invention into fashion in England and I should not fail to write to some of our doctors very particulary about it if I knew anyone of them that I thought had virtue enough to destroy such a considerable branch of their revenue for the good of mankind. But that distemper is too beneficial to them not to expose to all their resentment the hardy wight that should undertake to put an end to it. Perhaps, if I live to return, I may, however, have cour-age to war with them. Upon this occasion admire the heroism in the heart of your friend, etc.

Adrianople, 1 April 1718

To Anne Thistlethwayte,
I can now tell dear Mrs Thistelthwayte that I am safely
arrived at the end of my very long journey. I will not
tire you with the account of the many fatigues I have
suffered. You would rather hear something of what I
see here and a letter out of Turkey that has nothing
extraordinary in it would be as great a disappointment
as my visitors will receive at London, if I return thither
without any rarities to show them. What shall I tell
you of? You never saw camels in your life, and perhaps
the description of them will appear new to you. I can
assure you, the first sight of them was very much so to
me, and though I have seen hundreds of pictures of
those animals I never saw any that was resembling
enough to give me a true idea of them. I am going to
make a bold observation and possibly a false one,
because nobody has ever made it before me, but I do
take them to be of the stag kind; their legs, bodies and
necks are exactly shaped like them, and their colour
very near the same. 'Tis true they are much larger,
being a great deal higher than a horse, and so swift
that, after the defeat of Peterwardein, they far out-
ran the swiftest horses and brought the first news
of the loss of the battle to Belgrade. They are never
thoroughly tamed; the drivers take care to tie them one
to another with strong ropes, fifty in a string, led by an
ass on which the driver rides. I have seen three hundred
in one caravan. They carry the third part more than

any horse but 'tis a particular art to load them because of the bunch on their backs. They seem to me very ugly creatures, their heads being ill-formed and disproportioned to their bodies. They carry all the burdens, and the beasts destined to the plough are buffaloes, an animal you are also unacquainted with. They are larger and more clumsy than an ox. They have short black horns close to their heads, which grow turning backwards. They say this horn looks very beautiful when 'tis well polished. They are all black, with very short hair on their hides, and have extreme little white eyes that make them look like devils. The country people dye their tails and the hair of their foreheads red by way of ornament. Horses are not put here to any laborious work, nor are they at all fit for it. They are beautiful and full of spirit but generally little and not so strong as the breed of colder countries; very gentle, however, with all their vivacity, swift and sure-footed. I have a little white favourite that I would not part with on any terms. He prances under me with so much fire you would think that I had a great deal of courage to dare mount him. Yet I'll assure you I never rid a horse so much at my command. My side saddle is the first was ever seen in this part of the world and is gazed at with as much wonder as the ship of Columbus was in America. Here are some birds held in a sort of religious reverence and for that reason, multiply prodigiously: turtles [doves] on the account of their innocence and storks because they are supposed to make every winter the pilgrimage to Mecca. To say truth they are the happiest subjects under the Turkish government, and are so sensible of their privileges they walk the streets without fear and generally build in the low parts of houses. Happy are those that are so distinguished. The vulgar Turks are perfectly persuaded that they will not be that year attacked either by fire or pestilence. I have the happiness of one of their sacred nests under my chamber window.

Now I am talking of my chamber I remember the description of the houses here will be as new to you as any of the birds or beasts. I suppose you have read in most of our accounts of Turkey that their houses are the most miserable pieces of building in the world. I can speak very learnedly on that subject, having been in so many of them and I assure you 'tis no such thing. We are now lodged in a palace belonging to the Grand Signor. I really think the manner of building here very agreeable and proper for the country. 'Tis true, they are not at all solicitous to beautify the outsides of their houses and they are generally built of wood, which I own is the cause of many inconveniences, but this is not to be charged on the ill taste of the people, but on the oppression of the government. Every house, upon the death of its master, is at the Grand Signor's disposal and therefore no man cares to make a great expense which he is not sure his family will be the better for. All their design is to build a house commodious and that will last their lives, and they are very indifferent if it falls down the year after. Every house, great and small, is divided into two distinct parts, which only join together by a narrow passage. The first house has a large court before it, and open galleries all round it, which is to me a thing very agreeable. This gallery leads to all the chambers which are commonly large, and with two rows of windows, the first being of painted glass. They seldom build above two storeys, each of which has such galleries. The stairs are broad and not often above thirty steps. This is the house belonging to the lord, and the adjoining one is called the harem, that is, the ladies' apartment (for the name of seraglio is peculiar to the Grand Signor's). It has also a gallery running round it towards the garden to which all the windows are turned, and the same number of chambers as the other, but more gay and splendid, both in painting and furniture. The second row of windows are very low, with grates like those of convents.

The rooms are all spread with Persian carpets and raised at one end of them (my chamber is raised at both ends) about two feet. This is the sofa, and is laid with a richer sort of carpet, and all round it a sort of couch raised half a foot, covered with rich silk, according to the fancy or magnificence of the owner. Mine is of scarlet cloth with a gold fringe. Round about this are placed, standing against the wall, two rows of cushions, the first very large and the next little ones, and here the Turks display their greatest magnificence. They are generally brocade or embroidery of gold wire upon satin. Nothing can look more gay and splendid. These seats are so convenient and easy that I believe I shall never endure chairs as long as I live. The rooms are low, which I think no fault, the ceiling always of wood generally inlaid or painted and gilded. They use no hangings, the rooms being all wainscoted with cedar set off with silver nails or painted with flowers, which open in many places with folding doors and serve for cabinets, I think more conveniently than ours. Between the windows are little arches to set pots of perfume or baskets of flowers. But what pleases me best is the fashion of having marble fountains in the lower part of the room, which throws up several spouts of water giving, at the same time, an agreeable coolness and a pleasant dashing sound, falling from one basin to another. Some of these fountains are very magnificent. Each house has a bagnio, which consists generally in two or three little rooms, leaded on the top, paved with marble with basins, cocks of water, and all conveniences for either hot or cold baths.

You will perhaps be surprised at an account so different from what you have been entertained with by the common voyage writers, who are very fond of speaking of what they don't know. It must be under a very particular character, or on some extraordinary occasion when a Christian is admitted into the house of a man of quality, and their harems are always forbidden ground. Thus they can only speak of the outside, which makes no great appearance, and the women's apartments are always built backward, removed from sight, and have no other prospect than the gardens, which are enclosed with very high walls. There is none of our parterres in them, but they are planted with high trees which give an agreeable shade, and, to my fancy, a pleasing view. In the midst of the garden is the kiosk, that is, a large room commonly beautified with a fine fountain in the midst of it. It is raised nine or ten steps and enclosed with gilded lattices round which vines, jessamines and honeysuckles twining make a sort of green wall. Large trees are planted round this place, which is the scene of their greatest pleasures, and where the ladies spend most of their hours, employed by their music or embroidery. In the public gardens there are public kiosks where people go that are not so well accommodated at home, and drink their coffee, sherbet etc. Neither are they ignorant of a more durable manner of building. Their mosques are all of free stone, and the public hans or inns extremely magnificent, many of them taking up a large square built round with shops under stone arches, where poor artificers are lodged gratis. They have always a mosque joining to them, and the body of the han is a most noble hall, capable of holding three or four hundred persons, the court extreme spacious and cloisters round it that give it the air of our colleges. I own I think these foundations a more reasonable piece of charity than the founding of convents. I think I have now told you a great deal for once. If you don't like my choice of subjects, tell me what you would have me write upon. There is nobody more desirous to entertain you than, dear Mrs Thistlethwayte, etc.

Adrianople, 18 April 1718

To Lady Mar,
I writ to you, dear sister, and to all my other English correspondents, by the last ship and only heaven can

tell when I shall have another opportunity of sending to you; but I cannot forbear writing though perhaps my letter may lie upon my hands this two months. To confess the truth my head is so full of my entertainment yesterday that 'tis absolutely necessary for my own repose to give it some vent. Without farther preface, I will then begin my story.

I was invited to dine with the Grand Vizier's lady, and it was with a great deal of pleasure I prepared myself for an entertainment which was never given before to any Christian. I thought I should very little satisfy her curiosity, which I did not doubt was a considerable motive to the invitation, by going in a dress she was used to see, and therefore dressed myself in the court habit of Vienna, which is much more magnificent than ours. However, I chose to go incognito to avoid any disputes about ceremony, and went in a Turkish coach, only attended by my woman that held up my train and the Greek lady who was my interpretress. I was met at the court door by her black eunuch, who helped me out of the coach with great respect, and conducted me through several rooms, where her she-slaves, finely dressed, were ranged on each side. In the innermost I found the lady sitting on her sofa, in a sable vest. She advanced to meet me, and presented me half a dozen of her friends with great civility. She seemed a very good woman, near fifty years old. I was surprised to observe so little magnificence in her house, the furniture being all very moderate and, except the habits and number of her slaves, nothing about her that appeared expensive. She guessed at my thoughts and told me that she was no longer of an age to spend either her time or money in superfluities; that her whole expense was in charity, and her employment praying to God. There was no affectation in this speech; both she and her husband are entirely given up to devotion. He never looks upon any other woman and, what is much more extraordinary, touches no bribes, notwithstanding the example of all his predecessors. He is so scrupulous on this point, he would not accept Mr Wortley's present till he had been assured over and over that 'twas a settled perquisite of his place, at the entrance of every ambassador.

She entertained me with all kind of civility, till dinner came in, which was served, one dish at a time, to a vast number, all finely dressed after their manner, which I do not think so bad as you have perhaps heard it represented. I am a very good judge of their eating, having lived three weeks in the house of an *effendi* at Belgrade, who gave us very magnificent dinners, dressed by his own cooks which the first week pleased me extremely but, I own I then began to grow weary of it and desired our own cook might add a dish or two after our manner. But I attribute this to custom. I am very much inclined to believe an Indian that had never tasted of either, would prefer their cookery to ours. Their sauces are very high, all the roast very much done. They use a great deal of rich spice. The soup is served for the last dish and they have at least as great variety of ragouts as we have. I was very sorry I could not eat of as many as the good lady would have had me, who was very earnest in serving me of everything.

The treat concluded with coffee and perfumes, which is a high mark of respect; two slaves kneeling censed my hair, clothes and handkerchief. After this ceremony she commanded her slaves to play and dance, which they did with their guitars in their hands, and she excused to me their want of skill, saying she took no care to accomplish them in that art. I returned her thanks and, soon after took my leave.

I was conducted back in the same manner I entered and would have gone straight to my own house but the Greek lady with me earnestly solicited me to visit the Kabya's lady, saying he was the second officer in the empire and ought indeed to be looked upon as the first, the Grand Vizier having only the name, while he exercised the authority. I had found so little diversion in this harem that I had no mind to go into another. But her importunity prevailed with me and I am extremely glad I was so complaisant. All things here were with quite another air than at the Grand Vizier's and the very house confessed the difference between an old devote and a young beauty. It was nicely clean and magnificent. I was met at the door by two black eunuchs who led me through a long gallery between two ranks of beautiful young girls, with their hair finely plaited almost hanging to their feet, all dressed in fine light damasks brocaded with silver. I was sorry that decency did not permit me to stop to consider them nearer. But that thought was lost upon my entrance into a large room or rather pavilion built round with gilded sashes, which were most of them thrown up and the trees planted near them gave an agreeable shade which hindered the sun from being troublesome, the jessamines and honeysuckles that twisted round their trunks shedding a soft perfume, increased by a white marble fountain playing sweet water in the lower part of the room, which fell into three or four basins with a pleasing sound. The roof was painted with all sorts of flowers falling out to gilded baskets, that seemed tumbling down.

On a sofa raised three steps and covered with fine Persian carpets, sat the Kabya's lady, leaning on cushions of white satin, embroidered, and at her feet sat two young girls, the eldest about twelve year old, lovely as angels, dressed perfectly rich, and almost covered with jewels. But they were hardly seen near the fair Fatima (for that is her name) so much her beauty effaced everything I have seen all that has been called lovely either in England or Germany and must own that I never saw anything so gloriously beautiful, nor can I recollect a face that would have been taken notice of near hers. She stood up to receive me, saluting me after their fashion putting her hand upon her heart with a sweetness full of majesty that no court breeding could ever give. She ordered cushions to be given me and took care to place me in the corner, which is the place of honour. I confess, though, the Greek lady had before given me a great opinion of her beauty I was so struck with admiration that I could not for some time speak to her, being wholly taken up in gazing. That surprising harmony of features! That charming result of the whole! That exact proportion of body! That lovely bloom of complexion, unsullied by art! The unutterable enchantment of her smile! But her eyes! Large and black, with all the soft languishment of the blue! Every turn of her face discovering some new charm! After my first surprise was over I endeavoured, by nicely examining her face, to find out some imperfection, without any fruit of my search, but my being clearly convinced of the error of that vulgar notion, that a face perfectly regular would not be agreeable; nature having done for her, with more success, what Apelles is said to have essayed, by a collection of the most exact features, to form a perfect face. And to that a behaviour so full of grace and sweetness, such easy motions, with an air so majestic, yet free from stiffness or affectation that I am persuaded, could she be suddenly transported upon the most polite throne of Europe nobody would think her other than born and bred to be a queen, though educated in a country we call barbarous. To say all in a word, our most celebrated English beauties would vanish near her.

She was dressed in a caftan of gold brocade, flowered with silver, very well fitted to her shape, and showing to advantage the beauty of her bosom, only shaded by the thin gauze of her shift. Her drawers were pale pink, her waistcoat green and silver, her slippers white, finely embroidered, her lovely arms adorned with bracelets of diamonds and her broad girdle set round with diamonds; upon her head a rich Turkish handkerchief of pink and silver, her own fine black hair hanging a great length in various tresses, and on one side of her head some bodkins of jewels. I am afraid you will accuse me of extravagance in this description. I think I have read somewhere that women always speak in rapture when they speak of beauty, but I can't imagine why they should not be allowed to do so. I rather think it virtue to be able to admire without any mixture of desire or envy. The gravest writers have spoken with great warmth of some celebrated pictures and statues. The workmanship of Heaven certainly excels all our weak imitations, and I think has a much better claim to our praise. For my part I am not ashamed to own I took more pleasure in looking on the beauteous Fatima than the finest piece of sculpture could have given me. She told me the two girls at her feet were her daughters, though she appeared too young to be their mother.

Her fair maids were ranged below the sofa, to the number of twenty, and put me in mind of the pictures of the ancient nymphs. I did not think all nature could have furnished such a scene of beauty. She made them a sign to play and dance. Four of them immediately begun to play some soft airs on instruments, between a lute and a guitar, which they accompanied with their voices, while the others danced by turns. This dance was very different from what I had seen before. Nothing could be more artful or more proper to raise certain ideas; the tunes so soft, the motions so languishing, accompanied with pauses and dying eyes, half falling back and then recovering themselves in so artful a manner that I am very positive the coldest and most rigid prude upon earth could not have looked upon them without thinking of something not to be spoke of. I suppose you may have read that the Turks have no music but what is shocking to the ears, but this account is from those who never heard any but what is played in the streets, and is just as reasonable as if a foreigner should take his ideas of English music from the bladder and string or the marrow-bones and cleavers. I can assure you that the music is extremely pathetic; 'tis true, I am inclined to prefer the Italian, but perhaps I am partial. I am acquainted with a Greek lady who sings better than Mrs Robinson and is very well skilled in both, who gives the preference to the Turkish. 'Tis certain they have very fine natural voices; these were very agreeable.

When the dance was over, four fair slaves came into the room with silver censers in their hands and perfumed the air with amber, aloes wood and other scents. After this they served me coffee upon their knees in the finest japan china, with soucoups of silver gilt. The lovely Fatima entertained me all this while, in the most polite agreeable manner, calling me often güzel Sultanum, or the beautiful Sultana, and desiring my friendship with the best grace in the world, lamenting that she could not entertain me in my own language.

When I took my leave, two maids brought in a fine silver basket of embroidered handkerchiefs. She begged I would wear the richest for her sake and gave the others to my woman and interpretress. I retired through the same ceremonies as before, and could not help fancying I had been some time in Mohammed's paradise, so much was I charmed with what I had seen. I know not how the relation of it appears to you. I wish it may give you part of my pleasure for I would have my dear sister share in all the diversions of etc.

Adrianople, 17 May 1718

To Abbé Conti,

I am going to leave Adrianople and I would not do it without giving some account of all that is curious in it, which I have taken a great deal of pains to see. I will not trouble you with wise dissertations, whether or no this is the same city that was anciently called Orestesit or Oreste, which you know better than I do. It is now called from the Emperor Adrian [Hadrian] and was the first European seat of the Turkish empire, and has been the favourite residence of many sultans. Mehmed IV the father, and Mustafa, the brother of the reigning emperor were so fond of it that they wholly abandoned Constantinople, which humour so far exasperated the janissaries that it was a considerable motive to the rebellions which deposed them. Yet this man seems to love to keep his court here. I can give no reason for this partiality. 'Tis true, the situation is fine and the country all round very beautiful, but the air is extreme bad and the seraglio itself is not free from the ill effect of it. The town is said to be eight miles in compass; I suppose they reckon in the gardens. There are some good houses in it, I mean large ones, for the architecture of their palaces never makes any great show. It is now very full of people, but they are most of them such as follow the court or camp, and when they are removed, I am told, 'tis no populous city. The river Maritza (anciently the Hebrus) on which it is situated is dried up every summer, which contributes very much to make it unwholesome. It is now a very pleasant stream. There are two noble bridges built over it. I had the curiosity to go to see the Exchange in my Turkish dress which is disguise sufficient, yet I own I was not very easy when I saw it crowded with janissaries; but they dare not be rude to a woman and made way for me with as much respect as if I had been in my own figure. It is half a mile in length, the roof arched and kept extremely neat. It holds 365 shops furnished with all sorts of rich goods, exposed to sale in the same manner as at the New Exchange in London, but the pavement kept much neater and the shops all so clean they seemed just new painted. Idle people of all sorts walk here for their diversion, or amuse themselves with drinking coffee or sherbet, which is cried about as oranges and sweetmeats are in our playhouses.

I observed most of the rich tradesmen were Jews. That people are in incredible power in this country. They have many privileges above the natural Turks themselves and have formed a very considerable commonwealth here, being judged by their own laws and have drawn the whole trade of the empire into their hands, partly by the firm union amongst themselves and prevailing on the idle temper and want of industry of the Turks. Every pasha has his Jew who is his homme d'affaires. He is let into all his secrets and does all his business. No bargain is made, no bribe received, no merchandise disposed of but what passes through their hands. They are the physicians, the stewards and the interpreters of all the great men. You may judge how advantageous this is to a people who never fail to make use of the smallest advantages. They have found the secret of making themselves so necessary they are certain of the protection of the court whatever ministry is in power. Even the English, French and Italian merchants, who are sensible in their artifices are however forced to trust their affairs to their negotiation, nothing of trade being managed without them and the meanest amongst them is too important to be disobliged since the whole body take care of his interests with as much vigour as they would those of the most considerable of their members. They are many of them vastly rich but take care to make little public show of it, though they live in their houses in the utmost luxury and magnificence. This copious subject has drawn me from my description of the exchange founded by Ali Pasha, whose name it bears. Near it is the Shershi, a street of a mile in length, full of shops and all kind of fine merchandise but excessive dear, nothing being made here. It is covered on the top with boards to keep out the rain, that merchants may meet conveniently in all weathers. The Bedesten near it is another exchange, built upon pillars, where all sort of horse furniture is sold; glittering everywhere with gold, rich embroidery and jewels it makes a very agreeable show.

From this place I went in my Turkish coach to the camp, which is to move in a few days to the frontiers. The Sultan is already gone to his tents, and all his court. The appearance of them is indeed very magnificent. Those of the great men are rather like palaces than tents, taking up a great compass of ground and being divided into a vast number of apartments. They are all of green and the pashas of three tails have those ensigns of their power placed in a very conspicuous manner before their tents which are adorned on the top with gilded balls, more or less according to their different ranks. The ladies go in their coaches to see this camp as eagerly as ours did to that of Hyde Park, but 'tis easy to observe that the soldiers do not begin the campaign with any great cheerfulness. The war is a general grievance upon the people but particularly hard upon the tradesmen.

Now the Grand Signor is resolved to lead his army in person every company of them is obliged upon this occasion to make a present according to their ability. I took the pains of rising at six in the morning to see that ceremony, which did not however begin till eight. The Grand Signor was at the seraglio window to see the procession, which passed through all the principal streets. It was preceded by an *Effendi* mounted on a camel richly furnished, reading aloud the Alcoran, finely bound, laid upon a cushion. He was surrounded by a parcel of boys in white, singing some verses of it, followed by a man dressed in green boughs representing a clean husbandman sowing seed. After him several reapers with garlands of ears of corn, as Ceres is pictured, with scythes in their hands seeming to mow; then a little machine drawn by oxen, in which was a windmill and boys employed in grinding corn, followed by another machine drawn by buffaloes carrying an oven and two more boys, one employed in kneading the bread and another in drawing it out of the oven. These boys threw little cakes on both sides among the crowd and were followed by the whole company of bakers marching on foot, two and two, in their best clothes, with cakes, loaves, pasties and pies of all sorts on their heads; and after them two buffoons or jack puddings with their faces and clothes smeared with meal, who diverted the mob with their antick gestures. In the same manner followed all the companies of trade in their empire, the nobler sort such as jewellers, mercers etc. finely mounted and many of the pageants that represented their trades perfectly magnificent, amongst which the furriers' made one of the best figures, being a very large machine set round with the skins of ermines, foxes etc. so well stuffed the animals seemed to be alive, followed by music and dancers. I believe there were, upon the whole, at least 20,000 men, all ready to follow his highness if he commanded them.

The rear was closed by the volunteers who came to beg the honour of dying in his service. This part of the show seemed to me so barbarous I removed from the window upon the first appearance of it. They were all naked to the middle, their arms pierced through with arrows left sticking in them, others had them sticking in their heads, the blood trickling down their faces, and some slashed their arms with sharp knives, making the blood spout out upon those that stood near, and this is looked upon as an expression of their zeal for glory. I am told that some make use of it to advance their love, and when they are near the window where their mistress stands, all the women in town being veiled to see this spectacle, they stick another arrow for her sake, who gives some sign of approbation and encouragement to this gallantry. The whole show lasted near eight hours, to my great sorrow, who was heartily tired, though I was in the house of the widow of the Captain Pasha (Admiral), who refreshed me with coffee, sweetmeats, sherbet etc. with all possible civility.

I went two days after to see the mosque of Sultan Selim I, which is a building very well worth the curiosity of a traveller. I was dressed in my Turkish habit and admitted without scruple, though I believe they guessed who I was by the extreme officiousness of the door keeper to show me every part of it. It is situated very advantageously in the midst of the city and in the highest part, making a very noble show. The first court has four gates and the innermost, three. They are both of them surrounded with cloisters with marble pillars of the Ionic order, finely polished and of very lively colours, the whole pavement being white marble, the roof of the cloisters being divided into several cupelos or domes, leaded, with gilt balls on the top, in the midst of each four fine fountains of white marble; before the great gate of the mosque a portico with green marble pillars.

It has five gates, the body of the mosque being one prodigious dome. I understand so little of architecture I dare not pretend to speak of the proportions; it seemed to me very regular. This I am sure of, it is vastly high, and I thought it the noblest building I ever saw. It had two rows of marble galleries on pillars with marble balustrades, the pavement marble covered with Persian carpets, and in my opinion it is a great addition to its beauty that it is not divided into pews and encumbered with forms and benches like our churches, nor the pillars (which are most of them red and white marble) disfigured by the little tawdry images and pictures that give the Roman Catholic churches the air of toyshops. The walls seemed to me inlaid with such very lively colours in small flowers, I could not imagine what stones had been made use of, but, going nearer, I saw they were crusted with japan china [Iznik ceramic] which has a very beautiful effect. In the midst hung a vast lamp of silver gilt, besides which I do verily believe there was at least 2,000 of a lesser size. This must look very glorious when they are all lighted, but that being at night no women are suffered to enter. Under the large lamp is a great pulpit of carved wood gilt and just by it a fountain to wash, which you know is an essential part of their devotion. In one corner is a little gallery enclosed with gilded lattices for the Grand Signor; at the upper end a large niche very like an altar, raised two steps, covered with gold brocade, and standing before it two silver gilt candlesticks the height of a man and in them white wax candles as thick as a man's waist. The outside of the mosque is adorned with four towers vastly high, gilt on the top, from whence the imams call the people to prayers. I had the curiosity to go up one of them, which is contrived so artfully as to give surprise to all that see it. There is but one door which leads to three different staircases going to the three different storeys of the tower in such a manner that three priests may ascend rounding without ever meeting each other, a contrivance very much admired. Behind the mosque is an exchange full of shops where poor artificers are lodged gratis. I saw several dervishes at their prayers here. They are dressed in a plain piece of woollen with their arms bare and a woollen cap on their heads like a high crowned hat without brims. I went to see some other mosques built much after the same manner, but not comparable in point of magnificence to this I have described, which is infinitely beyond any church in Germany or England. I won't talk of other countries I have not seen. The seraglio does not seem a very magnificent palace, but the gardens very large, plentifully supplied with water and full of trees, which is all I know of them, never having been in them.

I tell you nothing of the order of Mr Wortley's entry and his audience. Those things are always the same and have been so often described I won't trouble you with the repetition. The young prince, about eleven year old sits near his father when he gives audience. He is a handsome boy, but probably will not immediately succeed the Sultan, there being two sons of Sultan Mustafa (his eldest brother) remaining, the eldest about 20 year old, on whom the hopes of the people are fixed. This reign has been bloody and avaricious. I am apt to believe they are very impatient to see the end of it. I am, sir, your etc.

I will write to you again from Constantinople.

Constantinople, 29 May 1717

To the Abbé Conti,

I have had the advantage of very fine weather all my journey and the summer being now in its beauty I enjoyed the pleasure of fine prospects; and the meadows being full of all sort of garden flowers and sweet herbs my berlin perfumed the air as it pressed them. The Grand Signor furnished us with thirty covered waggons for our baggage and five coaches of the country for my women. We found the road full of the great sipahis and their equipages coming out of Asia to the war. They always travel with tents, but I chose to lie in houses all the way. I will not trouble you with the names of the villages we passed in which there was nothing remarkable, but at Ciorlu we were lodged in a conac or little seraglio, built for the use of the Grand Signor when he goes this road. I had the curiosity to view all the apartments destined for the ladies of his court. They were in the midst of a thick grove of trees made fresh by fountains, but I was surprised to see the walls almost covered with little distiches of Turkish verse writ with pencils. I made my interpreter explain them to me and I found several of them very well turned, though I easily believed him that they lost much of their beauty in the translation. One runs literally thus in English:

We come into this world, we lodge, and we depart;
He never goes that's lodged within my heart.

The rest of our journey was through fine painted meadows by the side of the sea of Marmora, the ancient Propontis. We lay the next night at Selivrea, anciently a noble town. It is now a very good sea port, and neatly built enough, and has a bridge of thirty two arches. Here is a famous ancient Greek church. I had given one of my coaches to a Greek lady who desired the convenience of travelling with me. She designed to pay her devotions and I was glad of the opportunity of going with her. I found it an ill built place, set out with the same sort of ornaments but less rich than the Roman Catholic churches. They showed me a saint's body, where I threw a piece of money and a picture of the Virgin Mary drawn by the hand of St Luke, very little to the credit of his painting, but, however, the finest madonna of Italy is not more famous for her miracles. The Greeks have the most monstrous taste in their pictures, which for more finery are always drawn upon a gold ground. You may imagine what a good air this has, but they have no notion either of shade or proportion. They have a bishop here who officiated in his purple robe, and sent me a candle almost as big as myself for a present when I was at my lodging.

We lay the next night at a town called Büjük Cekmege or Great Bridge and the night following at Kujük Cekmege, Little Bridge, in a very pleasant lodging, formerly a monastery of dervishes, having before it a large court encompassed with marble cloisters with a good fountain in the middle. The prospect from this place and the gardens round it are the most agreeable I have seen, and shows that monks of all religions know how to choose their retirements. 'Tis now belonging to a *hogia* or school master, who teaches boys here, and asking him to show me his own apartment I was surprised to see him point to a tall cypress tree in the garden, on the top of which was a place for a bed for himself and a little lower one for his wife and two children who slept there every night. I was so much diverted with the fancy I resolved to examine his nest nearer but after going up fifty steps I found I had still fifty to go and then I must climb from branch to branch with some hazard of my neck. I thought it the best way to come down again.

We arrived the next evening at Constantinople, but I can yet tell you very little of it, all my time having been taken up with receiving visits, which are at least a very good entertainment to the eyes, the young women being all beauties and their beauty highly improved by the good taste of their dress. Our palace is in Pera, which is no more a suburb of Constantinople than Westminster is a suburb to London. All the Ambassadors are lodged very near each other. One part of our house shows us the port, the city and the seraglio and the distant hills of Asia, perhaps altogether the most beautiful prospect in the world. A certain French author says that Constantinople is twice as large as Paris. Mr Wortley is unwilling to own 'tis bigger than London, though I confess it appears to me to be so, but I don't believe 'tis so populous. The burying fields about it are certainly much larger than the whole city. 'Tis surprising what a vast deal of land is lost this way in Turkey. Sometimes I have seen burying places of several miles belonging to very inconsiderable villages which were formerly great towns and retain no other mark of their ancient grandeur. On no occasion they remove a stone that serves for a monument. Some of them are costly enough, being of a very fine marble. They set up a pillar with a carved turban on the top of it to the memory of a man and as the turbans by their different shapes show the quality or profession, 'tis in a manner putting up the arms of the deceased; besides, the pillar commonly bears a large inscription in gold letters. The ladies have a simple pillar without other ornament, except those that die unmarried who have a rose on top of it. The sepulchres of particular families are railed in and planted round with trees. Those of the sultans and some great men have lamps constantly burning in them.

When I spoke of their religion I forgot to mention two particularities, one of which I had read of, but it seemed so odd to me I could not believe it. Yet 'tis certainly true that when a man has divorced his wife in the most solemn manner he can take her again upon no other terms than permitting another man to pass a night with her, and there are some examples of those that have submitted to this law rather than not have back their beloved. The other point of doctrine is very extraordinary; any woman that dies unmarried is looked upon to die in a state of reprobation. To confirm this belief they reason that the end of the creation of woman is to increase and multiply, and she is only properly employed in the works of her calling when she is bringing children or taking care of them, which are all the virtues that God expects from her; and indeed, their way of life, which shuts them out of all public commerce, does not permit them any other. Our vulgar notion that they do not own women to have any souls is a mistake. 'Tis true they say they are not of so elevated a kind and therefore must not hope to be admitted into the paradise appointed for the men, who are to be entertained by celestial beauties, but there is a place of happiness destined for souls of the inferior order where all good women are to be in eternal bliss. Many of them are very superstitious and will not remain widows ten days for fear of dying in the reprobate state of a useless creature. But those that like their liberty and are not slaves to their religion content themselves with marrying when they are afraid of dying. This is a piece of theology very different from that which teaches nothing to be more acceptable to God than a vow of perpetual virginity. Which divinity is most rational I leave you to determine.

I have already made some progress in a collection of Greek medals. Here are several professed antiquaries who are ready to serve anybody that desires them, but you can't imagine how they stare in my face when I enquire about them, as if nobody was permitted to seek after medals till they were grown a piece of antiquity themselves. I have got some very valuable of the Macedonian kings, particularly one of Perseus, so lively I fancy I can see all his ill qualities in his face. I have a porphyry head finely cut of the true Greek sculpture, but who it represents is to be guessed at by the learned when I return, for you are not to suppose these antiquaries, who are all Greeks, know anything. Their trade is only to sell. They have correspondents at Aleppo, Grand Cairo, in Arabia and Palestine, who send them all they can find, and very often great heaps that are only fit to melt into pans and kettles. They get the best price they can for any of them, without knowing those that are valuable from those that are not. Those that pretend to skill generally find out the image of some saint in the medals of the Greek cities. One of them, showing me the figure of Pallas with a victory in her hand on a reverse, assured me it was the Virgin holding a crucifix. The same man offered me the head of a Socrates on a Sardonix, and to enhance the value gave him the title of St Augustine. I have bespoke a mummy, which I hope will come safe to my hands, notwithstanding the misfortune that befell a very fine one designed for the King of Sweden. He gave a great price for it, and the Turks took it into their heads that he must certainly have some considerable project depending upon it. They fancied it the body of God knows who and that the fate of their empire mystically depended on the conservation of it. Some old prophecies were remembered upon this occasion, and the mummy committed prisoner to the seven towers, where it has remained under close confinement ever since. I dare not try my interest in so considerable a point as the release of it, but I hope mine will pass without examination. I can tell you nothing more at present of this famous city. When I have looked a little about me you shall hear from me again. I am, sir, etc.

Belgrade Village [outside Istanbul], 17 June 1717

To Lady—,

I heartily beg your ladyship's pardon, but I really could not forbear laughing heartily at your letter and the commissions you are pleased to honour me with. You desire me to buy you a Greek slave who is to be mistress of a thousand good qualities. The Greeks are subjects and not slaves. Those who are to be bought in that manner are either such as are taken in war or stole by the Tartars from Russia, Circassia or Georgia, and are such miserable, awkward, poor wretches you would not think any of them worthy to be your housemaid. 'Tis true that many thousands were taken in the Morea, but they have been most of them redeemed by the charitable contributions of the Christians or ransomed by their own relations at Venice. The fine slaves that wait upon the great ladies or serve the pleasures of the great men are all bought at the age of eight or nine year old and educated with great care to accomplish them in singing, dancing, embroidery, etc. They are commonly Circassians and their patron never sells them except it is as a punishment for some very great fault. If ever they grow weary of them, they either present them to a friend or give them their freedoms. Those that are exposed to sale at the markets are always either guilty of some crime or so entirely worthless that they are of no use at all. I am afraid you'll doubt the truth of this account, which I own is very different from our common notions in England, but it is not less truth for all that.

Your whole letter is full of mistakes from one end to the other. I see you have taken your ideas of Turkey from that worthy author Dumont, who has writ with equal ignorance and confidence. 'Tis a particular pleasure to me here to read the voyages to the Levant, which are generally so far removed from truth and so full of absurdities I am very well diverted with them. They never fail to give you an account of the women, which 'tis certain they never saw, and talking very wisely of the genius of men, into whose company they are never admitted, and very often describe mosques which they dare not peep into. The Turks are very proud and will not converse with a stranger they are not assured is considerable in his own country. I speak of the men of distinction, for as to the ordinary fellows, you may imagine what ideas their conversation can give of the general genius of the people.

As to the Balm of Mecca, I will certainly send you some, but it is not so easily got as you suppose it and I cannot in conscience advise you to make use of it. I know not how it comes to have such universal applause. All the ladies of my acquaintance at London and Vienna have begged me to send pots of it to them. I have had a present of a small quantity (which I'll assure you is very valuable) of the best sort, and with great joy applied it to my face, expecting some wonderful effect to my advantage. The next morning the change indeed was wonderful; my face was swelled to a very extraordinary size and all over as red as my Lady—'s.

It remained in this lamentable state three days, during which you may be sure I passed my time very ill. I believed it would never be otherwise and to add to my mortification Mr Wortley reproached my indiscretion without ceasing. However, my face is since in statu quo. Nay, I am told by the ladies here that 'tis much mended by the operation, which I confess I cannot perceive in my looking glass. Indeed, if one was to form an opinion of this balm from their faces, one should think very well of it. They all make use of it and have the loveliest bloom in the world. For my part, I never intend to endure the pain of it again. Let my complexion take its natural course and decay in its own due time. I have very little esteem for medicines of this nature; but you do as you please, madam, only remember before you use it that your face will not be such as you'll care to show in the drawing room for some days after.

If one was to believe the women in this country, there is a surer way of making oneself beloved than by becoming handsome, though you know that's our method. But they pretend to the knowledge of secrets that by way of enchantment gives them the entire empire over whom they please. For me, that am not very apt to believe in wonders, I cannot find faith for this. I disputed the point last night with a lady who really talks very sensibly on any other subject, but she was downright angry with me that she did not perceive she had persuaded me of the truth of forty stories she told me of this kind, and at last mentioned several ridiculous marriages that there could be no other reason assigned for. I assured her that in England, where we were entirely ignorant of all magic, where the climate is not half so warm nor the women half so handsome, we were not without our ridiculous marriages, and that we did not look upon it as anything supernatural when a man played the fool for the sake of a woman. But my arguments could not convince her against, as she said, her certain knowledge, though she added that she scrupled making use of charms herself, but that she could do it whenever she pleased and, staring in my face said, with a very learned air, that no enchantments would have their effect upon me, and that there were some people exempt from their power, but very few. You may imagine how I laughed at this discourse, but all the women here are of the same opinion. They don't pretend to any commerce with the devil, but that there are certain compositions to inspire love. If one could send over a shipload of them I fancy it would be a very quick way of raising an estate. What would not some ladies of our acquaintance give for such merchandise?

Adieu my dear Lady—. I cannot conclude my letter with a subject that affords more delightful scenes to the imagination. I leave you to figure to yourself the extreme court that will be made to me at my return if my travels should furnish me with such a useful piece of learning. I am, dear madam, etc.

Pera, Constantinople, 4 January 1718

To Anne Thistlethwayte,
I am infinitely obliged to you, dear Mrs Thistlethwayte, for your entertaining letter. You are the only one of my correspondents that have judged right enough to think I would gladly be informed of the news amongst you. All the rest of them tell me, almost in the same words, that they suppose I know everything. Why they are pleased to suppose in this manner I can guess no reason except they are persuaded that the breed of Mohammed's pigeon still subsists in this country and that I receive supernatural intelligence. I wish I could return your goodness with some diverting accounts from hence, but I know not what part of the scenes here would gratify your curiosity or whether you have any curiosity at all for things so far distant. To say the truth I am at this present writing not very much turned for the recollection of what is diverting, my head being wholly filled with the preparations necessary for the increase of my family, which I expect every day. You may easily guess at my uneasy situation, but I am, however, in some degree comforted by the glory that accrues to me from it, and a reflection on the contempt I should otherwise fall under.

You won't know what to make of this speech, but in this country it is more despicable to be married and not fruitful than it is with us to be fruitful before marriage. They have a notion that whenever a woman leaves off bringing children, 'tis because she is too old for that business, whatever her face says to the contrary, and this opinion makes the ladies here so ready to make proofs of their youth (which is as necessary in order to be a received beauty as it is to show the roof of nobility to be admitted Knight of Malta) that they do not content themselves with using the natural means, but fly to all sort of quackeries to avoid the scandal of being past child bearing and often kill themselves by them. Without any exaggeration, all the women of my acquaintance that have been married ten year have twelve or thirteen children, and the old ones boast of having had five-and-twenty or thirty a-piece, and are respected according to the number they have produced. When they are with child 'tis their common expression to say they hope God will be so merciful to them to send two this time, and when I have asked them sometimes how they expected to provide for such a flock as they desire, they answer that the plague will certainly kill half of them, which, indeed, generally happens without much concern to the parents, who are satisfied with the vanity of having brought forth so plentifully. The French Ambassadress is forced to comply with this fashion as well as myself. She has not been here much above a year and has lain in once and is big again. What is most wonderful is the exemption they seem to enjoy from the curse entailed on the sex. They see all company the day of their delivery and at the fornight's end return visits, set out in their jewels and new clothes. I wish I may find the influence of the climate in this particular, but I fear I shall continue an English woman in that affair as well as I do in my dread of fire and plague, which are two things very little feared here, most families having had their houses burnt down once or twice, occasioned by their extraordinary way of warming themselves, which is neither by chimneys nor stoves but a certain machine called a *tandir*, the height of two foot, in the form of a table covered with a fine carpet or embroidery. This is made only of wood, and they put into it a small quantity of hot ashes and sit with their legs under the carpet. At this table they work, read and very often sleep, and if they chance to dream, kick down the *tandir* and the hot ashes commonly sets the house on fire. There was five hundred houses burnt in this manner about a fortnight ago, and I have seen several of the owners since who seem not at all moved at so common a misfortune. They put their goods into a bark [boat] and see their houses burn with great philosophy, their persons being very seldom endangered, having no stairs to descend.

But having entertained you with things I don't like, 'tis but just I should tell you something that pleases me. The climate is delightful in the extremist degree. I am now sitting, this present 4th of January, with the windows open, enjoying the warm shine of the sun, while you are freezing over a sad sea-coal fire, and my chamber is set out with carnations, roses and jonquils fresh from my garden. I am also charmed with many points of the Turkish law, to our shame be it spoken, better designed and better executed than ours, particularly the punishment of convicted liars (triumphant criminals in our country, God knows). They are burnt in the forehead with a hot iron, being proved the authors of any notorious falsehood. How many white foreheads should we see disfigured? How many fine gentlemen would be forced to wear their wigs as low as their eyebrows were this law in practice with us? I should go on to tell you many other parts of justice, but I must send for my midwife.

Pera, Constantinople, 10 March 1718

To Lady Mar,

I have not writ to you, dear sister, these many months; a great piece of self-denial, but I know not where to direct or what part of the world you were in. I have received no letter from you since your short note of April last in which you tell me that you are on the point of leaving England and promise me a direction for the place you stay in, but I have in vain expected it till now, and now I only learn from the Gazette that you are returned, which induces me to venture this letter to your house at London. I had rather ten of my letters should be lost than you imagine. I don't write and I think 'tis hard fortune if one in ten don't reach you. However, I am resolved to keep the copies as testimonies of my inclination to give you, to the utmost of my power, all the diverting part of my travels while you are exempt from all the fatigues and inconveniencies.

In the first place I wish you joy of your niece, for I was brought to bed of a daughter five weeks ago. I don't mention this as one of my diverting adventures, though I must own that it is not half so mortifying here as in England, there being as much difference as there is between a little cold in the head, which sometimes happens here, and the consumptive coughs so common in London. Nobody keeps their house a month for lying in, and I am not so fond of any of our customs to retain them when they are not necessary. I returned my visits at three weeks end, and about four days ago crossed the sea which divides this place from Constantinople to make a new one, where I had the good fortune to pick up many curiosities.

I went to see the Sultana Hafise, favourite of the last Emperor Mustafa, who, you know (or perhaps you don't know) was deposed by his brother the reigning Sultan, and died a few weeks after, being poisoned, as it was generally believed. This lady was immediately after his death saluted with an absolute order to leave the seraglio and choose herself a husband from the great men at the Port. I suppose you imagine her overjoyed at this proposal. Quite contrary. These women, who are called and esteem themselves queens, look upon this liberty as the greatest disgrace and affront that can happen to them. She threw herself at the Sultan's feet and begged him to poniard [stab] her rather than use his brother's widow with that contempt. She represented to him in agonies of sorrow that she was privileged from this misfortune by having brought five princes into the Ottoman family, but all the boys being dead and only one girl surviving this excuse was not received and she was compelled to make her choice.

She chose Bekir Effendi, then Secretary of State and above fourscore year old, to convince the world that she firmly intended to keep the vow she had made of never suffering a second husband to approach her bed, and since she must honour some subject so far as to be called his wife she would choose him as a mark of her gratitude, since it was he that had presented her at the age of ten year old to her lost lord. But she has never permitted him to pay her one visit, though it is now fifteen year she has been in his house, where she passes her time in uninterrupted mourning with a constancy very little known in Christendom, especially in a widow of twenty-one, for she is now but thirty-six. She has no black eunuchs for her guard, her husband being obliged to respect her as a queen and not enquire at all into what is done in her apartment, where I was led into a large room, with a sofa the whole length of it, adorned with white marble pillars like a ruelle, covered with a pale blue figured velvet on a silver ground, with cushions of the same, where I was desired to repose till the Sultana appeared, who had contrived this manner of reception to avoid rising up at my entrance, though she made me an inclination of her head when I rose up to her. I was very glad to observe a lady that had been distinguished by the favour of an emperor to whom beauties were every day presented from all parts of the world. But she did not seem to me to have ever been half so beautiful as the fair Fatima I saw at Adrianople, though she had the remains of a fine face more decayed by sorrow than time.

But her dress was something so surprisingly rich I

cannot forbear describing it to you. She wore a vest called *dolaman*, and which differs from a caftan by longer sleeves and folding over at the bottom. It was of purple cloth straight to her shape and thick set, on each side down to her feet and round the sleeves, with pearls of the best water, of the same size as their buttons commonly are. You must not suppose I mean as large as those of my Lord – but about the bigness of a pea; and to these buttons large loops of diamonds in the form of those gold loops so common upon birthday coats. This habit was tied at the waist with two large tassels of smaller pearl and round the arms embroidered with large diamonds; her shift fastened at the bosom with a great diamond shaped like a lozenge, her girdle as broad as the broadest English riband entirely covered with diamonds. Round her neck she wore three chains which reached to her knees, one of large pearl at the bottom of which hung a fine coloured emerald as big as a turkey egg, another consisting of two hundred emeralds close joined together, of the most lively green, perfectly matched, every one as large as a half crown piece and as thick as three crown pieces, and another of emeralds perfectly round. But her earrings eclipsed all the rest. They were two diamonds shaped exactly like pears, as large as a big hazelnut. Round her talpack she had four strings of pearl, the whitest and most perfect in the world, at least enough to make four necklaces every one as large as the Duchess of Marlborough's, and of the same size, fastened with two roses consisting of a large ruby for the middle stone and round them twenty drops of clean diamonds to each. Besides this, her headdress was covered with bodkins of emeralds and diamonds. She wore large diamond bracelets and had five rings on her fingers, all single diamonds, except Mr Pitt's the largest I ever saw in my life. 'Tis for the jewellers to compute the value of these things, but according to the common estimation of jewels in our part of the world, her whole dress must be worth above £100,000 sterling. This I am very sure of, that no European queen has half the quantity and the Empress's jewels, though very fine, would look very mean near hers.

She gave me a dinner of fifty dishes of meat, which, after their fashion, was placed on the table but one at a time, and was extremely tedious, but the magnificence of her table answered very well to that of her dress. The knives were of gold, the hafts set with diamonds, but the piece of luxury that grieved my eyes was the table cloth and napkins, which were all tiffany, embroidered with silks and gold in the finest manner in natural flowers. It was with the utmost regret that I made use of these costly napkins, as finely wrought as the finest handkerchiefs that ever came out of this country. You may be sure that they were entirely spoilt before dinner was over. The sherbet, which is the liquor they drink at meals, was served in china bowls, but the covers and salvers massy gold. After dinner water was brought in a gold basin and towels of the same kind of the napkins, which I very unwillingly wiped my hands upon, and coffee was served in china with gold soûcoupes.

The Sultana seemed in very good humour and talked

to me with the utmost civility. I did not omit this opportunity of learning all that I possibly could of the seraglio, which is so entirely unknown amongst us. She assured me that the story of the Sultan's throwing a handkerchief is altogether fabulous and the manner upon that occasion no other but that he send the Kuslir Aga to signify to the lady the honour he intends her. She is immediately complimented upon it by the others and led to the bath where she is perfumed and dressed in the most magnificent and becoming manner. The Emperor precedes his visit by a royal present and then comes into her apartment. Neither is there any such thing as her creeping in at the bed's feet. She said that the first he make choice of was always after the first in rank and not the mother of the eldest son, as other writers would make us believe. Sometimes the Sultan diverts himself in the company of all his ladies, who stand in a circle round him, and she confessed that they were ready to die with jealousy and envy of the happy she that he distinguished by any appearance of preference. But this seemed to me neither better nor worse than the circles in most courts where the glance of the monarch is watched and every smile waited for with impatience and envied by those that cannot obtain it.

She never mentioned the Sultan without tears in her eyes, yet she seemed very fond of the discourse. My past happiness (said she) appears a dream to me, yet I cannot forget that I was beloved by the greatest and most lovely of mankind. I was chose from all the rest to make all his campaigns with him. I would not survive him if I was not passionately fond of the princess, my daughter, yet all my tenderness for her was hardly enough to make me preserve my life when I lost him. I passed a whole twelvemonth without seeing the light. Time has softened my despair, yet I now pass some days every week in tears devoted to the memory of my Sultan. There was no affectation in these words. It was easy to see she was in a deep melancholy, though her good humour made her willing to divert me.

She asked me to walk in her garden, and one of her slaves immediately brought her a pelisse of rich brocade lined with sables. I waited on her into the garden, which had nothing in it remarkable but the fountains, and from thence she showed me all her apartments. In her bedchamber her toilet was displayed, consisting of two looking glasses, the frames covered with pearls, and her night *talpak* set with bodkins of jewels, and near it three vests of fine sables, every one of which is at least worth 1000 dollars, £200 English money. I don't doubt these rich habits were purposely placed in sight, but they seemed negligently thrown on the sofa. When I took my leave of her I was complimented with perfumes as at the Grand Vizier's and presented with a very fine embroidered handkerchief. Her slaves were to the number of thirty, besides ten little ones, the eldest not above seven year old. These were the most beautiful girls I ever saw, all richly dressed, and I observed that the Sultana took a great deal of pleasure in these lovely children, which is a vast expense, for there is not a handsome girl of that age to be bought under £100 sterling. They wore little garlands of flowers, and their own hair braided, which was all their head-dress, but their habits all of gold stuffs. These served her coffee kneeling, brought water when she washed, etc. 'Tis a great part of the business of the older slaves to take care of these girls, to learn them to embroider and serve them as carefully as if they were children of the family.

Now do I fancy that you imagine I have entertained you all this while with a relation that has, at least, received many embellishments from my hand. This is but too like, says you, the Arabian tales; these embroidered napkins, and a jewel as large as a turkey's egg! You forget, dear sister, those very tales were writ by an author of this country and, excepting the enchantments, are a real representation of the manners here. We travellers are in very hard circumstances. If we say nothing but what has been said before us we are dull and we have observed nothing. If we tell anything new, we are laughed at as fabulous and romantic, not allowing for the difference of ranks, which afford difference of company, more curiosity, or the changes of customs that happen every twenty year in every country. But people judge of travellers exactly with the same candour, good nature and impartiality they judge of their neighbours upon all occasions. For my part, if I live to return amongst you I am so well acquainted with the morals of all my dear friends and acquaintances that I am resolved to tell them nothing at all, to avoid the imputation, which their charity would certainly incline them to, of my telling too much. But I depend upon your knowing me enough to believe whatever I seriously assert for truth, though I give you leave to be surprised at an account so new to you. But what would you say if I told you that I have been in a harem where the winter apartment was wainscoted with inlaid work of mother of pearl, ivory of different colours and olive wood, exactly like the little boxes you have seen brought out of this country; and those rooms designed for summer, the walls all crusted with japan china, the roofs gilt and the floors spread with the finest Persian carpets. Yet there is nothing more true, such is the palace of my lovely friend, the fair Fatima, who I was acquainted with at Adrianople. I went to visit her yesterday and, if possible, she appeared to me handsomer than before. She met me at the door of her chamber and, giving me her hand with the best grace in the world: 'You Christian ladies,' said she with a smile that made her as handsome as an angel, 'have the reputation of inconstancy, and I did not expect, whatever goodness you expressed for me at Adrianople, that I should ever see you again; but I am now convinced that I have really the happiness of pleasing you, and if you knew how I speak of you amongst our ladies you would be assured that you do me justice if you think me your friend.' She placed me in the corner of the sofa and I spent the afternoon in her conversation with the greatest pleasure in the world.

The Sultana Hafise is what one would naturally expect to find a Turkish lady; willing to oblige, but not knowing how to go about it, and 'tis easy to see in her manner that she has lived excluded from the world. But Fatima has all the politeness and good breeding of a court, with an air that inspires at once respect and tenderness; and now I understand her language I find her wit as engaging as her beauty. She is very curious after the manners of other countries and has not that partiality for her own so common to little minds. A Greek that I carried with me who had never seen her before (nor could have been admitted now if she had not been in my train) showed that surprise at her beauty and manner which is unavoidable at the first sight, and said to me in Italian: 'This is no Turkish lady; she is certainly some Christian.' Fatima guessed she spoke of her and asked what she said. I would not have told, thinking she would have been no better pleased with the compliment than one of our court beauties to be told she had the air of a Turk. But the Greek lady told it her and she smiled, saying: 'It is not the first time I have heard so. My mother was a Poloneze taken at the Siege of Camieniec [Kamianets], and my father used to rally me, saying he believed his Christian wife had found some Christian gallant, for I had not the air of a Turkish girl.' I assured her that if all the Turkish ladies were like her, it was absolutely necessary to confine them from public view for the repose of mankind, and proceeded to tell her what a noise such a face as hers would make in London or Paris. 'I can't believe you', replied she agreeably; 'if beauty was so much valued in your country as you say they would never have suffered you to leave it.'

Perhaps, dear sister, you laugh at my vanity in repeating this compliment, but I only do it as I think it very well turned and give it you as an instance of the spirit of her conversation. Her house was magnificently furnished and very well fancied, her winter rooms being furnished with figured velvet on gold grounds, and those for summer with fine Indian quilting embroidered with gold. The houses of the great Turkish ladies are kept clean with as much nicety as those in Holland. This was situated in a high part of the town, and from the windows of her summer apartment we had the prospect of the sea and the islands and the Asian mountains. My letter is insensibly grown so long, I am ashamed of it. This is a very bad symptom. 'Tis well if I don't degenerate into a downright story teller. It may be our proverb that knowledge is no burden may be true to oneself, but knowing too much is very apt to make us troublesome to other people.

Constantinople, 10 April 1718

To Lady Bristol,
At length I have heard, for the first time from my dear Lady Bristol, this present 10th of April 1718. Yet I am persuaded you have had the goodness to write before, but I have had the ill fortune to lose your letters. Since my last I have stayed quietly at Constantinople, a city that I ought in conscience to give your ladyship a right notion of, since I know you can have none but what is partial and mistaken from the writings of travellers. 'Tis certain there are many people that pass years here in Pera without having ever seen it, and yet they all pretend to describe it.

Pera, Tophana and Galata, wholly inhabited by Frank Christians, and which together make the appearance of a very fine town, are divided from it by the sea, which is not above half so broad as the broadest part of the Thames, but the Christian men are loathe to hazard the adventures they sometimes meet with amongst the levents or seamen (worse monsters than our watermen) and the women must cover their faces to go there, which they have a perfect aversion to do. 'Tis true they wear veils in Pera, but they are such as only serve to show their beauty to more advantage, and which would not be permitted in Constantinople. Those reasons deter almost every creature from seeing it, and the French Ambassadress will return to France, I believe, without ever having been there. You'll wonder, madam, to hear me add that I have been there very often. The yasmak, or Turkish veil, is become not only very easy but agreeable to me, and if it was not, I would be content to endure some inconvenience to content a passion so powerful with me as curiosity; and indeed the pleasure of going in a barge to Chelsea is not comparable to that of rowing upon the canal of the sea here, where for twenty miles together down the Bosphorus the most beautiful variety of prospects present themselves. The Asian side is covered with fruit trees, villages and the most delightful landscapes in nature. On the European stands Constantinople, situated on seven hills. The unequal heights make it seem as large again as it is (though one of the largest cities in the world), showing an agreeable mixture of gardens, pine and cyprus trees, palaces, mosques and public buildings, raised one above another with as much beauty and appearance of symmetry as your ladyship ever saw in a cabinet adorned by the most skilful hands, jars showing themselves above jars, mixed with canisters, babies [cups] and candlesticks. This is a very odd comparison, but it gives me an exact image of the thing.

I have taken care to see as much of the seraglio as is to be seen. It is on a point of land running into the sea; a palace of prodigious extent, but very irregular, the gardens a large compass of ground full of high cypress trees, which is all I know of them, the buildings all of white stone, leaded on top, with gilded turrets and spires, which look very magnificent, and indeed I believe there is no Christian king's palace half so large. There are six large courts in it all built round and set with trees, having galleries of stone; one of these for the guard, another for the slaves, another for the officers of the kitchen, another for the stables, the fifth for the divan, the sixth for the apartment destined for audiences. On the ladies' side there is at least as many more, with distinct courts belonging to their eunuchs and attendants, their kitchens, etc.

The next remarkable structure is that of St Sophia, which it is very difficult to see. I was forced to send three times to the *Kaymakam* (the governor of the town), and he assembled the chief *effendis* or heads of the law and enquired of the *mufti* whether it was lawful to permit it. They passed some days in this important debate, but I insisting on my request, permission was granted. I can't be informed why the Turks are more delicate on the subject of this mosque than any of the others, where what Christian pleases may enter without scruple. I fancy they imagine that having been once consecrated, people on pretence of curiosity might profane it with prayers, particularly to those saints who are still very visible in mosaic work, and no other way defaced but by the decays of time, for 'tis absolutely false what is so universally asserted, that the Turks defaced all the images that they found in the city. The dome of St Sophia is said to be 113 foot diameter, built upon arches, sustained by vast pillars of marble, the pavement and staircase marble. There is two rows of galleries supported with pillars of particoloured marble, and the whole roof mosaic work, part of which decays very fast and drops down. They presented me a handful of it. The composition seems to me a sort of glass or that paste with which they make counterfeit jewels. They show here the tomb of the Emperor Constantine, for which they have a great veneration. This is a dull, imperfect description of this celebrated building, but I understand architecture so little that I am afraid of talking nonsense in endeavouring to speak of it particularly.

Perhaps I am in the wrong, but some Turkish mosques please me better. That of Sultan Suleiman is in an exact square with four fine towers on the angles, in the midst of a noble cupola supported with beautiful marble pillars, two lesser at the ends supported in the same manner, the pavement and gallery round the mosque of marble. Under the great cupola is a fountain adorned with such fine coloured pillars I can hardly think them natural marble. On one side is the pulpit of white marble, and on the other the little gallery for the Grand Signor. A fine staircase leads to it and it is built up with gilded lattices. At the upper end is a sort of altar where the name of God is written, and before it stands two candlesticks as high as a man, with wax candles as thick as three flambeaux. The pavement is spread with fine carpets and the mosque illuminated with a vast number of lamps. The court leading to it is very spacious, with galleries of marble with green fountains covered with twenty-eight leaded cupolas on two sides, a fine fountain of three basins in the midst of it. The description may serve for all the mosques in Constantinople; the model is exactly the same, and they only differ in largeness and richness of materials. That of the Validé is the largest of all, built entirely of marble, the most prodigious and, I think, the most beautiful structure I ever saw, be it spoke to the honour of our sex, for it was founded by the mother of Mohammed IV. Between friends, St Paul's Church would make a pitiful figure near it, as any of our squares would do near the Atmeydan, or Place of Horses, 'at' signifying horse in Turkish.

This was the Hippodrome in the reign of the Greek emperors. In the midst of it is a brazen column of three serpents twisted together with their mouths gaping. 'Tis impossible to learn why so odd a pillar was erected; the Greeks can tell nothing but fabulous legends when they are asked the meaning of it, and there is no sign of its having ever had any inscription. At the upper end is an obelisk of porphyry, probably brought from Egypt, the hieroglyphics all very entire, which I look upon as mere ancient puns. It is placed on four little brazen pillars upon a pedestal of square free stone full of figures in bas relief on two sides, one square representing a battle, another an assembly. The others have inscriptions in Greek and Latin.

[. . .]

All the figures have their heads on, and I cannot forbear reflecting again on the impudence of authors who all say they have not, but I dare swear the greatest part of them never saw them, but took the report from the Greeks, who resist with incredible fortitude the conviction of their own eyes whenever they have invented lies to the dishonour of their enemies. Were you to ask them, there is nothing worth seeing in Constantinople but St Sophia, though there are several larger mosques. That of Sultan Achmed has that of particular, its gates are of brass. In all these mosques there are little chapels where are the tombs of the founders and their families, with vast candles burning before them.

The exchanges are all noble buildings, full of fine alleys, the greatest part supported with pillars, and kept wonderfully neat. Every trade has their distinct alley, the merchandise disposed in the same order as in the New Exchange at London. The Bedesten, or jewellers' quarter shows so much riches, such a vast quantity of diamonds and all kind of precious stones, that they dazzle the sight. The embroiderers' is also very glittering, and people walk here as much for diversion as business. The markets are most of them handsome squares, and admirably well provided, perhaps better than in any other part of the world. I know you'll expect I should say something particular of that of the slaves, and you will imagine me half a Turk when I don't speak of it with the same horror other Christians have done before me, but I cannot forbear applauding the humanity of the Turks to those creatures. They are never ill used and their slavery is in my opinion no worse than servitude all over the world. 'Tis true they have no wages, but they give them yearly clothes to a higher value than our salaries to any ordinary servant. But you'll object men buy women with an eye to evil. In my opinion they are bought and sold as publicly and more infamously in all our Christian great cities. I must add to the description of Constantinople that the Historical Pillar is no more, dropped down about two year before I came. I have seen no other footsteps of antiquity, except the aqueducts, which are so vast that I am apt to believe they are yet ancienter than the Greek Empire, though the Turks have clapped in some stones with Turkish inscription to give their nation the honour of so great a work, but the deceit is easily discovered.

The other public buildings are the hans and monasteries, the first very large and numerous, the second few in number and not at all magnificent. I had the curiosity to visit one of them and observe the devotions of the dervishes, which are as whimsical as any in Rome. These fellows have permission to marry, but are confined to an odd habit, which is only a piece of coarse white cloth wrapped about them, with their legs and arms naked. Their order has few other rules, except that of performing their fantastic rites every Tuesday and Friday, which is in this manner. They meet together in a large hall, where they all stand, with their eyes fixed on the ground and their arms across, while the imam or preacher reads part of the Alcoran from a pulpit placed in the midst; and when he has done, eight or ten of them make a melancholy consort with their pipes, which are no unmusical instruments. Then he reads again and makes a short exposition on what he has read, after which they sing and play till their superior (the only one of them dressed in green) rises and begins a sort of solemn dance. They all stand about him in a regular figure, and while some play the others tie their robe, which is very wide, fast round their waists and begin to turn round with an amazing swiftness and yet with great regard to the music, moving slower or faster as the tune is played. This lasts above an hour without any of them showing the least appearance of giddiness, which is not to be wondered at when it is considered they are all used to it from infancy, most of them being devoted to this way of life from their birth, and sons of dervishes. There turned amongst them some little dervishes of six or seven years old who seem no more disordered by that exercise than the others. At the end of the ceremony they shout out; 'there is no other god but God, and Mohammed is his prophet', after which they kiss the superior's hand and retire. The whole is performed with the most solemn gravity. Nothing can be more austere than the form of these people. They never raise their eyes and seem devoted

to contemplation, and as ridiculous as this is in description there is something touching in the air of
submission and mortification they assume.

This letter is of a horrible length but you may burn
it when you have read enough.

Mr Wortley is not yet here, but I may assure your
ladyship in his name of the respect he has for you. I
give humble service to my Lord Bristol and Mr Hervey.

Pera, Constantinople, May 1718

To the Countess of—,
Your ladyship may be assured I received yours with
very great pleasure. I am very glad to hear that our
friends are in good health, particularly Mr Congreve,
who I heard was ill of the gout. I am now preparing to
leave Constantinople, and perhaps you will accuse me
of hypocrisy when I tell you 'tis with regret, but I am
used to the air and have learnt the language. I am easy
here, and as much as I love travelling, I tremble at the
inconveniences attending so great a journey with a
numerous family and a little infant hanging at the
breast. However, I endeavour upon this occasion to do
as I have hitherto done in all the odd turns of my life;
turn them, if I can, to my diversion. In order to do
this, I ramble every day, wrapped up in my ferace and
yasmak about Constantinople and amuse myself with
seeing all that is curious in it. I know you'll expect this
declaration should be followed with some account of
what I have seen, but I am in no humour to copy what

has been writ so often over. To what purpose should I tell you that Constantinople was the ancient Byzantium, that 'tis at present the conquest of a race of people supposed Scythians, that there is five or six thousand mosques in it, that St Sophia was founded by Justinian etc? I'll assure you 'tis not want of learning that I forbear writing all these bright things. I could also, with little trouble, turn over Knolles and Sir Paul Rycaut to give you a list of Turkish emperors, but I will not tell you what you may find in every author that has writ of this country.

I am more inclined, out of a true female spirit of contradiction, to tell you the falsehood of a great part of what you find in authors; as, for example, the admirable Mr Hill, who so gravely asserts that he saw in St Sophia a sweating pillar very balsamic for disordered heads. There is not the least tradition of any such matter, and I suppose it was revealed to him in vision during his wonderful stay in the Egyptian catacombs, for I am sure he never heard of any such miracle here. 'Tis also very pleasant to observe how tenderly he and all his brethren voyage-writers lament on the miserable confinement of the Turkish ladies, who are, perhaps, freer than any ladies in the universe, and are the only women in the world that lead a life of uninterrupted pleasure, exempt from cares, their whole time being spent in visiting, bathing or the agreeable amusement of spending money and inventing new fashions. A husband would be thought mad that exacted any degree of economy from his wife, whose expenses are no way limited but by her own fancy. 'Tis his business to get money and hers to spend it, and this noble prerogative extends itself to the very meanest of the sex. Here is a fellow that carries embroidered handkerchiefs upon his back to sell, as miserable a figure as you may suppose such a mean dealer, yet I'll assure you his wife scorns to wear anything less than cloth of gold, has her ermine furs and a very handsome set of jewels for her head. They go abroad when and where they please. 'Tis true they have no public places but the bagnios, and there can only be seen by their own sex. However, that is a diversion they take great pleasure in.

I was three days ago at one of the finest in the town and had the opportunity of seeing a Turkish bride received there and all the ceremonies used on that occasion, which made me recollect the epithalamium of Helen by Theocritus, and it seems to me that the same customs have continued ever since. All the she-friends, relations and acquaintance of the two families newly allied meet at the bagnio. Several others go out of curiosity and I believe there was that day at least 200 women. Those that were or had been married placed themselves round the room on the marble sofas, but the virgins very hastily threw off their clothes and appeared without other ornament or covering than their own long hair braided with pearl or ribbon. Two of them met the bride at the door, conducted by her mother and another grave relation. She was a beautiful maid of about seventeen, richly dressed and shining with jewels, but was presently reduced by them to the state of nature. Two others filled silver gilt pots with perfume and begun the procession, the rest following in pairs to the number of thirty. The leaders sung an epithalamium answered by the others in chorus, and the two last led the fair bride, her eyes fixed on the ground with a charming affectation of modesty. In this order they marched round the three large rooms of the bagnio. 'Tis not easy to represent to you the beauty of this sight, most of them being well proportioned and white skinned, all of them perfectly smooth and polished by the frequent use of bathing. After having made their tour, the bride was again led to every matron round the rooms, who saluted her with a compliment and a present, some of jewels, others pieces of stuff, handkerchiefs, or little gallantries of that nature, which she thanked them for by kissing their hands.

I was very well pleased with having seen this ceremony and you may believe me that the Turkish ladies have at least as much wit and civility, nay, liberty, as ladies amongst us. 'Tis true the same customs that give them so many opportunities of gratifying their evil inclinations (if they have any) also puts it very fully in the power of their husbands to revenge them if they are discovered, and I don't doubt but they suffer sometimes for their indiscretions in a very severe manner. About two months ago there was found at daybreak not very far from my house the bleeding body of a young woman, naked, only wrapped in a course sheet, with two wounds with a knife, one in her side and another in her breast. She was not yet quite cold, and so surprisingly beautiful that there were very few men in Pera that did not go to look upon her, but it was not possible for anybody to know her, no woman's face being known. She was supposed to be brought in dead of night from the Constantinople side and laid there. Very little enquiry was made about the murderer and the corpse privately buried without noise. Murder is never pursued by the king's officers as with us. 'Tis the business of the next relations to revenge the dead person, and if they like better to compound the matter for money, as they generally do, there is no more said of it. One would imagine this defect in their government should make such tragedies very frequent, yet they are extremely rare, which is enough to prove the people not naturally cruel, neither do I think in many other particulars they deserve the barbarous character we give them.

I am well acquainted with a Christian woman of quality who made it her choice to live with a Turkish husband, and is a very agreeable sensible lady. Her story is so extraordinary I cannot forbear relating it, but I promise you it shall be in as few words as I can possibly express it. She is a Spaniard, and was at Naples with her family when that Kingdom was part of the Spanish dominion. Coming from thence in a felucca, accompanied by her brother they were attacked by the Turkish Admiral, boarded and taken; and now how shall I modestly tell you the rest of her adventure? The same accident happened to her that happened to the fair Lucretia so many years before her, but she was too good a Christian to kill herself as that heathenish Roman did. The admiral was so much charmed with the beauty and long suffering of the fair captive that as his first compliment he gave immediate liberty to her brother and attendants, who made haste to Spain and in a few months sent the sum of £4000 sterling as a ransom for his sister. The Turk took the money, which he presented to her, and told her she was at liberty, but the lady very discreetly weighted the different treatment she was likely to find in her native country. Her Catholics relations, as the kindest thing they could do for her in her present circumstances, would certainly confine her to a nunnery for the rest of her days. Her infidel lover was very handsome, very tender, fond of her and lavished at her feet all the Turkish magnificence. She answered him very resolutely that her liberty was not so precious to her as her honour, that he could no way restore that but by marrying her. She desired him to accept the ransom as her portion and give her the satisfaction of knowing no man could boast of her favours without being her husband. The Admiral was transported at this kind offer and sent back the money to her relations, saying he was too happy in her possession. He married her and never took any other wife, and (as she says herself) she never had any reason to repent the choice she made. He left her some years after one of the richest widows in Constantinople, but there is no remaining honourably a single woman, and that consideration has obliged her to marry the present Captain Pasha (ie Admiral), his successor. I am afraid you'll think that my friend fell in love with her ravisher, but I am willing to take her word for it that she acted wholly on principles of honour, though I think she might be reasonably touched at his generosity, which is very often found amongst Turks of rank.

'Tis a degree of generosity to tell the truth, and 'tis very rare that any Turk will assert a solemn falsehood. I don't speak of the lowest sort, for as there is a great deal of ignorance, there is very little virtue amongst them, and false witnesses are much cheaper than in Christendom, those wretches not being punished (even when they are publicly detected) with the rigour they ought to be. Now I am speaking of their law, I don't know whether I have ever mentioned to you one custom peculiar to this country. I mean adoption, very common amongst the Turks and yet more amongst the Greeks and Armenians. Not having it in their power to give their estates to a friend or distant relation to avoid its falling into the Grand Signor's treasury, when they are not likely to have children of their own they choose some pretty child of either sex amongst the meanest people and carry the child and its parents before the *cadi*, and there declare they receive it for their heir. The parents at the same time renounce all future claim to it, a writing is drawn and witnessed and a child thus adopted cannot be disinherited. Yet I have seen some common beggars that have refused to part with their children in this manner to some of the richest amongst the Greeks, so powerful is the instinctive fondness natural to parents! Though the adopting fathers are generally very tender to these children of their souls, as they call them. I own this custom pleases me much better than our absurd following our name. Methinks 'tis much more reasonable to make happy and rich an infant whom I educate after my own manner, brought up, in the Turkish phrase, upon my knees, and who has learnt to look upon me with a filial respect, than to give an estate to a creature without other merit or relation to me than by a few letters. Yet this is an absurdity we see frequently practised.

Now I have mentioned the Armenians, perhaps it will be agreeable to tell you something of that nation, with which I am sure you are utterly unacquainted. I will not trouble you with the geographical account of the situation of their country, which you may see in the map, or a relation of their ancient greatness, which you may read in the Roman history. They are now subject to the Turks, and, being very industrious in trade, and increasing and multiplying, are dispersed in great numbers through all the Turkish dominions. They were, as they say, converted to the Christian religion by St Gregory, and are perhaps the devoutest Christians in the whole world. The chief precepts of their priests enjoin the strict keeping of their Lents, which are at least seven months in every year, and are not to be dispensed with on the most emergent necessity. No occasion whatever can excuse them if they touch anything more than mere herbs or roots, without oil, and plain dry bread. This is their Lenten diet. Mr Wortley has one of his interpreters of this nation, and the poor fellow was brought so low with the severity of his fasts that his life was despaired of, yet neither his master's commands or the doctor's entreaties (who declared nothing else could save his life) were powerful enough to prevail with him to take two or three spoonfuls of broth. Excepting this, which may rather be called custom than an article of faith, I see very little in their religion different from ours. 'Tis true they seem to incline very much to Mr Whiston's doctrine, neither do I think the Greek church very distant from it, since 'tis certain the insisting on the Holy Spirit only proceeding from the Father is making a plain subordination in the Son. But the Armenians have no notion of transubstantiation, whatever account Sir Paul Rycaut gives of them (which account I am apt to believe was designed to compliment our court in 1679), and they have a great horror for those amongst them that change to the Roman religion.

What is most extraordinary in their customs is their matrimony, a ceremony I believe unparalleled all over the world. They are always promised very young, but the espoused never see one another till three days after their marriage. The bride is carried to church with a cap on her head in the fashion of a large trencher, and over it a red silken veil which covers her all over to her feet. The priest asks the bridegroom whether he is contented to marry that woman, be she deaf, be she blind. These are the literal words, to which having answered yes, she is led home to his house accompanied with all the friends and relations on both sides, singing and dancing, and is placed on a cushion in the corner of the sofa, but her veil never lifted up, not even by her husband, till she has been three days married. There is something so odd and monstrous in these ways that I could not believe them till I had enquired of several Armenians myself who all assured me of the truth of them, particularly one young fellow who wept when he spoke of it, being promised by his mother to a girl that he must marry in this manner, though he protested to me he had rather die than submit to this slavery, having already figured his bride to himself with all the deformities in nature.

I fancy I see you bless yourself at this terrible relation. I cannot conclude my letter with a more surprising story, yet 'tis as seriously true as that I am, dear sister, your etc.

Pera, Constantinople, 19 May 1718

To the Abbé Conti,

I am extremely pleased with hearing from you, and my vanity (the darling frailty of humankind) not a little flattered by the uncommon questions you ask me, though I am utterly incapable of answering them, and indeed were I as good a mathematician as Euclid himself, it requires an age's stay to make just observations on the air and vapours.

I have not been yet a full year here and am on the point of removing; such is my rambling destiny. This will surprise you, and can surprise nobody so much as myself. Perhaps you will accuse me of laziness of dulness, or both together, that can leave this place without giving you some account of the Turkish court. I can only tell you that if you please to read Sir Paul Rycaut you will there find a full and true account of the viziers, the Berglerbleys, the civil and spiritual government, the officers of the seraglio, etc., things that 'tis very easy to procure lists of and therefore may be depended on, though other stories, God knows – I say no more – everybody is at liberty to write their own remarks. The manners of people may change or some of them escaped the observation of travellers, but 'tis not the same of the government, and for that reason, since I can tell you nothing new I will tell nothing of it. In the same silence shall be passed over the arsenal and seven towers, and for the mosques, I have already described one of the noblest to you very particularly; but I cannot forbear taking notice to you of a mistake of Gemelli (though I honour him in a much higher degree than any other voyage-writer). He says that there is no remains of Calcedon. This is certainly a mistake. I was there yesterday and went cross the canal in my galley, the sea being very narrow between that city and Constantinople, 'Tis still a large town and has several mosques in it. The Christians still call it Calcedonia, and the Turks give it a name I forgot, but which is only a corruption of the same word [Kadikoy]. I suppose this an error of his guide, which his short stay hindered him from rectifying, for I have, in other matters, a very just esteem for his veracity.

Nothing can be pleasanter than the canal, and the Turks are so well acquainted with its beauties, all their pleasure seats are built on its banks, where they have at the same time the most beautiful prospects in Europe and Asia. There are near one another some hundreds of magnificent palaces. Human grandeur being here yet more unstable than anywhere else, 'tis common for the heirs of a great three-tailed pasha not to be rich enough to keep in repair the house he built; thus in a

few years they all fall to ruin. I was yesterday to see
that of the late Grand Vizier who was killed at Peterwardein. It was built to receive his royal bride, daughter
of the present Sultan, but he did not live to see her
there. I have a great mind to describe it to you, but I
check that inclination, knowing very well that I cannot
give you, with my best description, such an idea of it
as I ought. It is situated on one of the most delightful
parts of the canal, with a fine wood on the side of a hill
behind it. The extent of it is prodigious; the guardian
assured me there is 800 rooms in it. I will not answer
for that number since I did not count them, but 'tis
certain the number is very large and the whole adorned
with a profusion of marble, gilding and the most
exquisite painting of fruit and flowers. The windows
are all sashed with the finest crystalline glass brought
from England, and all the expensive magnificence that
you can suppose in a palace founded by a vain young
luxurious man with the wealth of a vast empire at his
command. But no part of it pleased me better than the
apartments destined for the bagnios. There are two
exactly built in the same manner, answering to one
another; the baths, fountains and pavements all of
white marble, the roofs gilt and the walls covered with
japan china; but adjoining to them two rooms, the
upper part of which is divided into a sofa; in the four
corners falls of water from the very roof, from shell to
shell of white marble to the lower end of the room,
where it falls into a large basin surrounded with pipes
that throw up the water as high as the room. The walls
are in the nature of lattices and on the outside of them

vines and woodbines planted that form a sort of green tapestry and give an agreeable obscurity to these delightful chambers. I should go on and let you into some of the other apartments, all worthy your curiosity, but 'tis yet harder to describe a Turkish palace than any other, being built entirely irregular. There is nothing can be properly called front or wings, and though such a confusion is, I think, pleasing to the sight, yet it would be very unintelligible in a letter. I shall only add that the chamber destined for the Sultan, when he visits his daughter, is wainscotted with mother of pearl fastened with emeralds like nails; there are others of mother of pearl and olive wood inlaid, and several of japan china. The galleries, which are numerous and very large, are adorned with jars of flowers and porcelain dishes of fruit of all sorts, so well done in plaster and coloured in so lively a manner that it has an enchanting effect. The garden is suitable to the house, where arbours, fountains and walks are thrown together in an agreeable confusion. There is no ornament wanting except that of statues.

Thus you see, sir, these people are not so unpolished as we represent them. 'Tis true their magnificence is of a different taste from ours, and perhaps of a better. I am almost of opinion they have a right notion of life; while they consume it in music, gardens, wine and delicate eating, while we are tormenting our brains with some scheme of politics or studying some science to which we can never attain, or if we do, cannot persuade people to set that value upon it we do ourselves, 'Tis certain what we feel and see is properly (if anything is properly) our own, but the good of fame, the folly of praise, hardly purchased, and when obtained, poor recompense for loss of time and health! We die, or grow old and decrepit before we can reap the fruit of our labours. Considering what short lived, weak animals men are, is there any study so beneficial as the study of present pleasure? I dare not pursue this then; perhaps I have already said too much, but I depend upon the true knowledge you have of my heart. I don't expect from you the insipid railleries I should suffer from another in answer to this letter. You know how to divide the idea of pleasure from that of vice, and they are only mingled in the heads of fools – but I allow you to laugh at me for the sensual declaration that I had rather be a rich *effendi* with all his ignorance than Sir Isaac Newton with all his knowledge. I am, sir, etc.

Dover, 31 October 1718

To the Abbé Conti,
I am willing to take your word for it that I shall really oblige you by letting you know as soon as possible my safe passage over the water. I arrived this morning at Dover after being tossed a whole night in the packet boat in so violent a manner that the master, considering the weakness of his vessel, thought it prudent to remove the mail, and gave us notice of the danger. We called a little fisher boat, which could hardly make up to us, while all the people on board us were crying to heaven,

and 'tis hard to imagine oneself in a scene of greater horror than on such an occasion; and yet, shall I own it to you, though I was not at all willing to be drowned, I could not forbear being entertained at the double distress of a fellow passenger? She was an English lady that I had met at Calais, who desired me to let her go over with me in my cabin. She had bought a fine point head [cap] which she was contriving to conceal from the custom house officers. When the wind grew high and our little vessel cracked, she fell very heartily to her prayers and thought wholly of her soul. When it seemed to abate she returned to the worldly care of her headdress, and addressed herself to me. 'Dear madam, will you take care of this point? If it should be lost . . . ah Lord! We shall all be lost! Lord have mercy on my soul. Pray, madam, take care of this headdress'. This easy transition from her soul to her headdress, and the alternate agonies that both gave her, made it hard to determine which she thought of greatest value. But, however, the scene was not so diverting but I was glad to get rid of it and be thrown into the little boat, though with some hazard of breaking my neck. It brought me safe hither and I cannot help looking with partial eyes on my native land. That partiality was certainly given us by nature to prevent rambling, the effect of an ambitious thirst after knowledge which we are not formed to enjoy. All we get by it is fruitless desire of mixing the different pleasures and conveniences which are given to different parts of the world and cannot meet in any one of them. After having read all that is to be found in the languages I am mistress of, and having decayed my sight by midnight studies, I envy the easy peace of mind of a ruddy milk maid who, undisturbed by doubt, hears the sermon with humility every Sunday, having not confused the sentiments of natural duty in her head by the vain enquiries of the schools, who may be more learned, yet after all must remain as ignorant. And, after having seen part of Asia and Africa and almost made the tour of Europe, I think the honest English squire more happy who verily believes the Greek wines less delicious than March beer, that the African fruits have not so fine a flavour as golden pippins, and the becáfiguas of Italy are not so well tasted as a rump of beef, and that, in short, there is no perfect enjoyment of this life out of Old England. I pray God I may think so for the rest of my life, and since I must be contented with our scanty allowance of daylight, that I may forget the enlivening sun of Constantinople.